THE CENTER

For Reference

Not to be taken from this room

THE

CENTER

A Guide to Genealogical Research in the National Capital Area

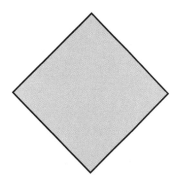

Christina K. Schaefer

Previous editions of this work were published under
the title *Lest We Forget: A Guide to Genealogical
Research in the Nation's Capital.*

Contents

Preface

The Annandale Family History Center of the Church of Jesus Christ of Latter-day Saints published the first edition of *Lest We Forget: A Guide to Genealogical Research in the Nation's Capital* in 1965. Editors of the first and subsequent editions focused on providing detailed information on the resources of the National Archives, the Library of Congress, and the library of the National Society of the Daughters of the American Revolution. The work was unique in its attempt to guide researchers through the maze of agencies, departments, archives, and record groups in some large and rather intimidating institutions. I extend my gratitude and respect to the editors of all the editions of *Lest We Forget*: June A. Babbel, Colleen S. Neal, and H. Byron Hall.

The Center: A Guide to Genealogical Research in the National Capital Area is a new work in which I try to keep the purpose of *Lest We Forget* alive while at the same time expanding its coverage and, hopefully, its usefulness. With the arrival of the communications revolution, it is now relatively easy to access the catalogs and even some of the holdings of the well-known institutions described here, but this book is still needed to understand precisely what genealogical resources are available in the nation's capital and where they can be found.

Various people helped me in the preparation of this book, and I am grateful to all of them. I would like to thank Constance S. OConnell for her assistance in research and editing in chapter 2. Staff members of the Annandale Family History Center who conferred on the manuscript are Linda Adamo, Lynne Gregory, Margaret Hawk, Thomas Petersen, Victoria Robinson, and Delores Taylor. From the Family History Department in Salt Lake City I am grateful to Jayare Roberts, A.G., M.L.S., of Family History Center Support.

Individuals at the facilities described in this book who provided information and assistance are: Dr. Ira Glazier, Balch Institute, Center for Immigration Research; Constance S. OConnell, Daughters of the American Revolution; Judith P. Austin, Library of Congress; Constance Potter, National Archives; and John Peterson, National Park Service.

I could not have written this book without the support of my husband, Doug, and my children Alice and Eric.

My special appreciation goes to Michael Tepper, my editor, who has taught me to be a better writer.

Christina K. Schaefer, C.G.R.S.
June 1996

THE CENTER

Chapter 1
Where Do I Start?

"No nation had ever before the opportunity offered them of deliberately deciding the spot where their Capital City should be fixed . . . the plan should be drawn on such a scale as to leave room for that aggrandizement, an embellishment which the increase of the wealth of the nation, will permit it to pursue at any period, however remote."

Pierre Charles L'Enfant to George Washington, 1789 (Quoted in *An Illustrated History of the City of Washington,* by the Junior League of Washington, edited by Thomas Froeneck. Avenel, NJ: Wings Books, 1977, p. 46).

Over two hundred years later, the City of Washington in the Federal District of Columbia stands as the center of government of the most powerful and culturally diverse country in the world. From its very conception, Washington, DC had been envisioned as a center of knowledge and as a receptacle for the vast bodies of information it continues to accumulate. Its diamond shape is a metaphor for the priceless records housed here—treasures of U.S. and world history. From the great documents of government to the common citizen enumerated on a census record, the voices and lives of millions are the genealogical treasures of humankind's heritage.

Washington, DC is home to the largest body of accessible research materials in the world. The varied and far-ranging variety of resources in the national capital area are a mine of information for a researcher in any discipline. For the genealogical researcher, the most important aspects are the extensive selection of primary source documents and records, and the centralization of millions of books, manuscripts, maps, and other publications in repositories. In addition to government agencies, there are many private associations and special interest groups that are willing to help researchers. Moreover, most foreign governments maintain a diplomatic or economic office or organization in Washington. Most of these can provide information regarding access to sources in the countries that they represent.

About This Book

The purpose of this book is to identify those resources in the Washington, DC area that will aid genealogists and family historians to identify and trace their ancestors. Besides traditional sources of information, emphasis in this book is placed on the following:

→ Departments and agencies of the federal government
→ Regional, state, county, and local government institutions
→ Societies and associations with genealogical holdings
→ Ethnic, cultural, and religious groups that have libraries or services to the public
→ Colleges, universities, and private libraries with biographical and genealogical data
→ Family History Centers of the Church of Jesus Christ of Latter-day Saints

Special attention has been given to the most important research facilities, especially archives and libraries of the U.S. government. Currently, the National Archives and Records Administration (NARA) and the Library of Congress are undergoing renovation or reorganization. The Library is restoring the Thomas Jefferson Building and estimates its completion sometime in 1997. NARA has been relocating record groups among its centers, and is reportedly

A FOUR-GENERATION AMERICAN FAMILY, ca. 1895

close to the end of this project. As things change, it is probable that some of the reading and research rooms may move within their present locations.

The Gathering Process

With the advent of the "Information Age," research has become faster, broader, and, most importantly, more accessible. Some aspects of family history research can be conducted without leaving home. Online computer services, e-mail, fax modems, and optical disks provide instant access to millions of resources. For those who have microform readers, there are purchase and rental programs widely available.

The Family History Library of the Church of Jesus Christ of Latter-day Saints has established about 2,500 Family History Centers (see chapter 10) around the world. They have the FamilySearch® program on CD-ROM, and a circulating microfilm program for use in centers. Patrons can search records that, in the past, would have been impossible to access due to restrictions or prohibitive travel costs.

Some things, however, still require a research trip. With the concentration of sources available within a day's drive, many genealogists carefully plan their visit to the DC metro area. Societies and organizations frequently sponsor group visits, arranging transportation and travel in one easy package. Whether setting off alone or in a group, the key to any successful trip is to organize and set attainable goals in order of priority. Certain steps should be followed:

1. *Has all current research been carried to completion and organized on group sheets or in a computer genealogy program?*

The beginning researcher should attempt to uncover everything possible from family sources, including photos, vital records, newspaper clippings, and family journals. Even an older relative's address book or Christmas card register can provide vital leads for lost connections. Maps of the search areas can be reduced by section and carried in notebooks for ready reference. Organizing the information into a compact, portable file system or in a notebook

computer saves hours of valuable time at the research site.

2. *What information is missing?*

Identifying the holes in a family history is essential to making the best use of time on a research trip. Finding a missing marriage record or the date and place of immigration, or determining when a family moved from one U.S. state to another are all reasonable goals.

3. *Where can the missing information be found?*

There are several excellent handbooks and manuals on genealogical research. The most useful in this case would be those that indicate the kind of information found in different record sources, as well as those that give agency names, addresses, and phone numbers.

The best known handbooks are:

Bentley, Elizabeth P. *The Genealogist's Address Book.* 3rd ed. (Baltimore: Genealogical Publishing Co., 1995).

Eichholz, Alice, ed. *Ancestry's Red Book.* Revised Edition (Salt Lake City: Ancestry, 1992).

Greenwood, Val. *The Researcher's Guide to American Genealogy.* 2nd ed. (Baltimore: Genealogical Publishing Co., 1990).

The Handy Book for Genealogists: United States of America. 8th ed. (Logan, UT: Everton Publishers, Inc., 1991).

Kemp, Thomas J. *International Vital Records Handbook.* 3rd ed. (Baltimore: Genealogical Publishing Co., 1994).

---

4. *What work can be done in advance?*

Anything that can be obtained by mail or electronic means, or reviewed on microform ahead of time, avoids wasting travel time. Reviewing indexes in advance to determine the availability of a church record, deed, will, military service record, etc., usually will narrow the search to find out if a copy of the record can be obtained by mail, or may give clues for additional places to search.

5. *How can a researcher make the best use of a facility with genealogical records?*

Learning how to use any facility in advance will take a lot of frustration out of a trip. Most institutions will respond to written queries about holdings, policies, access, etc.

✓ If using a laptop or notebook computer, make sure the batteries are fully charged. Only a few facilities provide extra electrical outlets for patrons.

✓ Ready-made worksheets and forms make abstracting records more time-effective. Some researchers design their own forms; there are also many styles that are commercially available.

✓ When researching on site, always speak to the reference librarian to get the best information on available resources.

✓ Watch your valuables! Do not leave purses or briefcases unattended. Streamline briefcases and tote bags to carry a minimum of lightweight essentials.

✓ Remember to bring a supply of pencils and erasers, as some places do not allow pens. Other useful supplies are paper clips, a mini-stapler, post-it notes (not for use on documents), a glue stick, a pencil sharpener, and a magnifying glass.

✓ Have enough cash for photocopies, parking, vending machines, bus fare, etc. District of Columbia buses require exact change.

Books to help plan a research trip:

Balhuzen, Anne Ross. *Searching On Location: Planning a Research Trip* (Salt Lake City: Ancestry, 1992).

Mann, Thomas. *A Guide to Library Research Methods* (New York: Oxford University Press, 1987).

Neagles, James C. and Mark C. Neagles. *The Library of Congress: A Guide to Genealogical and Historical Research* (Salt Lake City: Ancestry, 1990).

Price, Robert L., ed. *The Washington Post Guide to Washington.* 2nd ed. (New York: McGraw Hill, 1989).

Ross, Betty. *Washington, DC Museums: A Ross Guide* (Washington, DC: Americana Press, 1992).

Whiteley, Sandy, ed. *American Library Association Guide to Information Access* (New York: Random House, 1994).

Getting Around

The streets in the District of Columbia are laid out to traverse in three directions —diagonally, east to west, and north to south. They are named this way:

☞ North to south: numerical names, i.e., 17th Street, NW
☞ East to west: alphabetical names, i.e., M Street, SE
☞ Diagonally: state names, i.e., Michigan Avenue, NE

A compact street atlas that fits neatly into a briefcase is *ADC's Pocket Atlas of Washington, DC, and Vicinity.* 2nd ed. (Alexandria, VA: ADC of Alexandria, n.d.). For more information, call 800-ADC-MAPS. It includes information on hospitals, points of interest, public transportation, and shopping.

Due to limited parking, public transportation is almost a must. The Metro system of subways and buses is the preferred means of travel. Taxicab fares are based on a zone system. Fares into Maryland and Virginia can be expensive. Private vehicles are a better alternative for visiting facilities outside of the Metro system.

Many resources, such as the National Genealogical Society, the U.S. Geological Survey Library, National Archives and Records Administration Suburban Annex, and all Family History Centers are outside of Washington, DC, in Virginia and Maryland.

The Interstate System

I-95 runs north to south from Baltimore to Richmond on the Maryland side of the District of Columbia.

I-495 "The Beltway" loops around DC to the west. The local area is frequently referred to as "inside" or "outside" the Beltway. The inner loop of I-495 runs clockwise, the outer loop counterclockwise. It is the easiest route to get from Maryland and Virginia, and vice versa.

I-395 "The Shirley Highway" is the main commuter route from Virginia into the District. It provides access to the Pentagon Metro Station, which has free parking after 2:00 PM weekdays, and all day on weekends and federal holidays.

I-295 is the major commuting route from Maryland into the District. To the north, it becomes the Baltimore-Washington Parkway (starting outside the Beltway).

I-66 is the east-west corridor from Prince William County, Virginia to the District.

1-270 carries all traffic from Frederick and Montgomery counties in Maryland to the District.

Dulles Toll Road runs from Dulles Airport in Loudon County, Virginia to the District.

U.S. Route 50 is the original east-west road through the District. It becomes New York Avenue.

U.S. Route 301 "The Old Tobacco Road" was the old stage coach road from Annapolis, MD to Richmond, VA that skirts the District. It is an alternate to I-95.

WARNING! The rush hour in the DC Metro commuting area is very heavy. Morning hours run from 5:30–9:30 AM and afternoon hours from 3:30–7:30 PM. Whenever possible, try to use public transportation during these hours.

Transportation Phone Numbers

Airport Information:
- Baltimore-Washington (BWI) 410-859-7111
- Dulles 703-661-2700
- National 703-419-7000

Amtrak 800-872-7245

Fairfax City CUE Bus 703-385-7859

Fairfax County, VA Bus System 703-385-7859

MARC commuter trains 800-325-7245

Metrorail/Metrobus 202-637-7000
- Free maps depicting streets and Metro subway routes 202-724-4091

Montgomery County, MD Bus System 301-217-7433

Prince George's County, MD Bus System 301-925-5656

Taxi Information:
- Capital Cab 202-546-2400
- Checker Cab 202-398-0531
- Diamond Cab 202-387-6200
- Yellow Cab 202-544-1212

VRE (Virginia Railway Express) 800-828-1120

Other Useful Phone Numbers

International Visitors Information Service (IVIS):45 language phone bank 202-783-6540

Lost or stolen travelers checks . . . . American Express 800-221-7182; Visa 800-227-5960

Police (non-emergency) District of Columbia 202-727-1010

Emergency: Police, Fire, Ambulance 911

Washington Convention and Visitors Association 202-789-1600

Time 202-844-2525

Weather 202-936-1212

Chapter 2

National Archives and Records Administration (NARA)

National Archives, "ARCHIVES I"
National Archives at College Park (NAACP), "ARCHIVES II"

Introduction

Use NARA records if it is known when, where, or how a person came into contact with the United States government. If they were counted in a census, performed military service, immigrated to the United States, or purchased land, check the National Archives and Records Administration's holdings. These include census, military service and pension, passenger arrival, and federal land records. The *Guide to Genealogical Research in the National Archives* (Washington, DC: National Archives Trust Fund Board, 1985) describes the research potential of NARA records.

The National Archives has made numerous changes in the locations of its holdings. Most of the records of genealogical value held by the National Archives will remain at Archives I. All the land, bounty land, U.S. Court of Claims records, U.S. District Court records, and passport applications that are at the Regional Records Center at Suitland, MD, will be relocated to Archives I. While in transition, some record groups may be closed. If in doubt as to where to find a record group, contact the genealogy staff of the Archives at 202-501-5410.

The buildings that have been closed, or are closing, and the agencies that have relocated, are:

→   Cartographic Branch of the National Archives in Alexandria, VA, **now closed**.
→   National Archives Regional Records Center, Suitland, MD, **closing by December 1996**.

☞ Locations
The National Archives Building, Archives I, is at 8th and Pennsylvania Avenue, NW, Washington, DC. Most genealogical research will be at this location.

The National Archives at College Park, Archives II, is at 8601 Adelphi Road in College Park, MD. Chapter 3 details the maps available at this facility that were originally held by the Cartographic Branch in Alexandria, VA.

☎ Phone Numbers, Archives I
User services: 202-501-5400
Genealogy consultants: 202-501-5410
Microfilm room: 202-501-5412
Military reference: 202-501-5385

🕒 Hours
Research Rooms
8:45 AM–5 PM Mon and Wed
8:45 AM–9 PM Tue, Thu, and Fri
8:45 AM–4:45 PM Sat

♿ Public Transportation and Parking
Archives I, Metro: The Archives/Navy Memorial stop on the Yellow and Green Lines of the Metro, Washington's subway, is across Pennsylvania Avenue from the Archives building.

Parking: Several commercial parking lots are also located nearby.

Archives II, Metro: Prince George's Plaza stop on the Green Line connects to a free shuttle bus that departs from the Belcrest Road side of the station, on a regular schedule, for Archives II.

Parking: Free researcher parking is available in the parking garage adjacent to the facility.

NATIONAL ARCHIVES

A shuttle service runs hourly between Archives I and Archives II.

→ Public Access
A picture ID is needed to enter each building. All personal belongings (except a wallet) must be put in a locker before entering a research room where original documents are being used. Use only pencils; notepaper is provided.

Personal computers may be used in all research rooms. Optical scanners are not permitted.

Register upon entering each room. Microfilm readers are assigned. Obtain and refile film rolls one at a time. Operating directions are on each machine. Always rewind film.

To use original records, such as Civil War military pensions, you must register for a NARA Researcher ID card in Room G-7. This card is valid for two years. At the College Park facility, ask the guard where to obtain an ID card.

Children under sixteen are not admitted to some areas.

→ Photoduplication
A debit card must be purchased to use in microfilm reader/printers and photocopiers (bills only). Copiers are self-service.

❖ Online Services
Several publications as text-based information are now available on Internet:
Point your gopher client at: gopher:// gopher.nara.gov/.
Using an HTTP client, such as mosaic:
The URL to use is http://www.nara.gov/.
Several publications are available through the NARA Fax-on-Demand System, 301-713-6905. You must call from a fax machine to receive documents.
Use e-mail to inquire @nara.gov.User Services

✎ Mail Requests
There are fill-in forms for requesting different types of information:

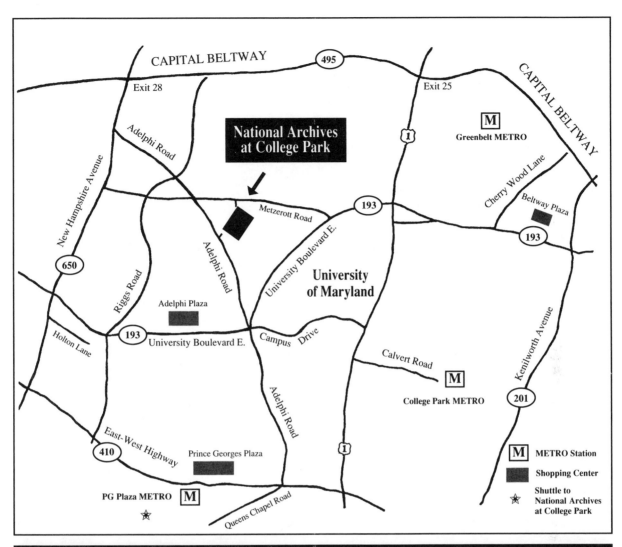

CAPITAL BELTWAY

495

Exit 28

Exit 25

M
Greenbelt METRO

Adelphi Road

National Archives
at College Park

New Hampshire Avenue

Cherry Wood Lane

Beltway Plaza

Metzerott Road

193

193

650

Adelphi Road

University Boulevard E.

University
of Maryland

Kenilworth Avenue

Riggs Road

Adelphi Plaza

Holton Lane

193

University Boulevard E.

Campus Drive

Calvert Road

M
College Park METRO

201

Adelphi Road

East-West Highway

410

Prince Georges Plaza

1

M METRO Station

Shopping Center

PG Plaza METRO M

☆

Queens Chapel Road

☆ Shuttle to
National Archives
at College Park

DIRECTIONS TO NATIONAL ARCHIVES FACILITIES IN THE WASHINGTON, DC, AREA

★ NATF Form 82 for census records.
★ NATF Form 80 for military records.
★ NATF Form 81 for passenger records.

To request forms, write to:
National Archives and Records Administration
8th and Pennsylvania Avenue, NW
Washington, DC 20408
Copies of these forms are also provided in the
Appendix to this volume.

Census searches are no longer done by Archives
staff in response to mail requests. However, if
you can specify the year, state, county, township or city/ward, and page number you want

from a particular census, the Archives will make
a copy for you.

Pension/Bounty Land Warrant Records
Request NATF Form 80, "Order for Copies of
Veterans Records." Fill out and return the form
along with the proper fee (currently $10). Re-
quest only one file per form. Selected documents will be sent to you. If the information
you want is not in the material sent to you,
inquire about the cost of obtaining copies of
the remaining documents in the file. In addition to a War of 1812 pension index search,
you can request an unindexed bounty land
search if you can provide the veteran's name,
state of service, and unit.

Army Service Records
Use NATF Form 80. When requesting Civil War Union service records, you must specify the state from which the veteran served, as there is no consolidated index. There is a consolidated index for Confederate service records.

Navy Service Records
Use NATF Form 80. Records available include those for enlisted personnel to 1885 and officers to 1902. There are no compiled service records for Navy personnel. However, a limited search will be made if you provide the following information:

✓ Name of veteran
✓ Name of war or dates of service
✓ Name of at least one vessel on which veteran served and dates of service
✓ Place of enlistment

Passenger Arrival Records
Request NATF Form 81, "Order for Copies of Ship Passenger Arrival Records." You must know the full name of the person, the port of arrival, and the approximate date of arrival. For periods where there are no indexes, you must have the full name of the person, the port of arrival, date of arrival, and the name of the ship. Request only one search per form.

Reproduction Services for Non-Textual Records
Reproduction work in both the Still Picture and the Cartographic branches has been turned over to several private vendors. Work stations have been established at Archives II at which the vendors handle all requests for reproduction, including digital copies on disk. The average turn-around time on an order is two weeks.

A catalog of all items available by mail is available upon request. Write to:

National Archives Trust Fund
NEPS Dept. 735
P.O.Box 100793
Atlanta, GA 30384

✍ Publications
Room G-9 at the Pennsylvania Avenue building, which is open weekdays 9:00 AM–4:30 PM, offers both free and for sale publications, including the following:

★   *Guide to Genealogical Research in the National Archives*
★   *Catalog of National Archives Microfilm Publications*
★   Select Catalogs of National Archives Microfilm Publications:
        American Indians
        Black Studies
        Genealogical and Biographical Research
        Immigrant and Passenger Arrivals
        Military Service Records
★   Preliminary Inventories
★   Special Lists
★   Microfilm Publication Number Pamphlets

Record group, filming, and roll numbers in this chapter are cited from the above sources.

✍ Microfilm Rental Program
More than 6,000 libraries through their inter-library loan divisions participate in this National Archives Microfilm Rental Program. Call 301-604-3699.

→ Food, Beverages, and Patron Services
Lockers are available in the second and fourth floor hallways. Snack bar and change machines are in the basement level. Public telephones and restrooms are in basement, second, and fourth floors.

Room 401 has an informative orientation slide program. To assist visitors, there are "Getting started . . ." information sheets on the fourth floor.

Both Archives I and II offer tours of their facilities. Archives II tours are held on Tuesday and Thursday at 10:15 AM and 1:15 PM. Archives I tours are given daily at the same times. Reservations can be made by calling the Volunteer Office at 202-501-5205.

General Information

<u>Record Group (RG)</u>
Each federal agency's records are designated a "record group" with a name and a number. Records are not arranged according to subject.

<u>Series (M or T)</u>
A "series" is a group of related documents within a record group. Each series of NARA records has been assigned a Microfilm Publication Number. For most of the M numbered series the Archives has a descriptive pamphlet (DP) available that explains the origin, content, and arrangement of the records. There is a roll number list for the M and the T numbered series. Consult the DP or the lists for the specific record needed, then check the Roll Location Guides in Room 400.

<u>Inventories and Preliminary Inventories (P)</u>
Some record groups have a finding aid called an "inventory" or "preliminary inventory." The inventory's description of records includes:

- ✓   name of the series
- ✓   series number
- ✓   length of time covered by the records
- ✓   amount of records
- ✓   arrangement of the records
- ✓   what information the records contain
- ✓   type of record: map, photograph, letter, etc.

<u>Special List (SL)</u>
A "special list" is a finding aid that gives a detailed description of the contents of a record series or a series of units of records.

<u>Box List</u>
"Box lists" are unpublished preliminary inventories that were created to assist in locating records of large record series.

There are different types of finding aids for each record group. Several have been published and are available free, and some must be purchased. Some of the aids are unpublished and can be requested at the information desk.

Room 400, Microfilm Reading Room

Upon entering Room 400 you will find:

- ★   Registration desk
- ★   Federal census population reports, 1790–1920
- ★   Self-service microfilm and microfiche copiers
- ★   Descriptive pamphlets and other lists of roll breaks for microfilm
- ★   Self-service photocopier
- ★   County census records
- ★   Bulk copier for microfilm
- ★   Adjutant General reports; Civil War pension indexes

<u>Stack Area</u>
The microfilm storage room contains:

- ★   Civil War records
- ★   Immigration records
- ★   Military records
- ★   Military pension indexes
- ★   Naturalization records
- ★   Non-population census schedules
- ★   *Papers of the Continental Congress*
- ★   Passenger lists

To use the films in the stack area you must know the microfilm publication number and the stack area location.

<u>The Finding Aids Room</u>
Room 402 contains a variety of genealogical research aids, including the following:

- ★   Passenger list aids and book indexes, including P. William Filby and Mary Meyer's *Passenger and Immigration Lists Index* (3 vols. plus Supplements)
- ★   1850, 1860, and 1870 township census listings
- ★   *1880 Enumeration District* descriptive books
- ★   *1910 City Enumeration District Index* State census indexes
- ★   Map cases and atlases
- ★   Lippincott's *Gazetteer*

The large atlas gives township and range numbers, which are necessary in using land records and in determining the name of a township when only the range and township numbers are given in the census records.

Roll Location Guide

The Roll Location Guides in Room 400 are arranged by microfilm publication number. The M publications are listed before the T publication numbers. Each entry gives the microfilm publication number, location in Room 400, title, dates of records, and number of roll.

The location has two numbers; for example, 075-06 means that the microfilm is found in cabinet 75 in drawer 6. Consult the descriptive pamphlets (M numbers) or lists (T numbers) to determine which roll you need. Remember the cabinet and drawer where the film was stored as it needs to be refiled when you are finished.

Room 203, Central Research Room

Procedure

Put your belongings, including coats, hats, briefcases, purses, and notebooks in the lockers on the second floor. The locker takes a quarter, which is returned when you empty the locker. Paper is provided in the research room.

At the guard desk show your National Archives Researcher ID card and sign in. Go to the main desk in Room 203 and ask for the records you previously requested. The records will be filed under your last name.

You may look at only one set of records at a time. Each set of records must be signed out with both the time and your initials noted on the pink slip. This pink slip is kept at the main desk until you return the records. Leave the green reference service slip with the box, volume, or packet. This slip is necessary for proper refiling.

When you have finished your research, sign the records back in, noting the return time and indicating if you are finished with the records. At your request the records will be held at the main desk for up to one week.

When the records are turned in and returned to the stack area, they cannot be retrieved again until they have been refiled. Records are held for three working days. If the records are not used for three working days, they are returned to the custodial unit for refiling.

When you are ready to leave, note the time in the register at the guard desk. The guard will examine all of your papers. Retrieve your belongings from the locker room.

Handling Historic Records

Records used in the National Archives research room are unique and require extra care when they are handled.

➤ Use records from one box and one file unit at a time.

➤ Retain all unbound records in their existing order.

➤ Replace records in the same order and facing in the same direction as originally found.

➤ Make notes only in pencil on paper provided by the National Archives.

➤ Make no marks of any kind on the records.

➤ Place nothing on top of the records. Take notes on paper placed beside the records.

➤ Have the staff examine all records before making reproductions and after the copies are made.

➤ Return all records to the file unit before leaving your study station temporarily.

The Reference Library in the Central Research Room is not a genealogical facility. Its subject emphasis is U.S. history, federal agency administration history, and archival theory. The card catalog is located in the Central Research Room. Among the Reference Library holdings are the following:

★ *Journals of the Continental Congress*
★ *The Papers of the Continental Congress*
★ *Territorial Papers of the U.S.*
★ *American State Papers*
★ *U.S. Official Register* (Civil War)
★ Dyer's *Compendium of the War of Rebellion*

★   *Congressional Record*
★   Papers of the State Department
★   Various "Who's Who" collections
★   General books on each U.S. war
★   Revolutionary War published records and rosters from Alabama, Georgia, Maine, Massachusetts, New Hampshire, New Jersey, New York, Pennsylvania, Texas, and Virginia
★   War of 1812 published records and rosters
★   Civil War compiled volumes, including adjutant general reports (soldier's name, rank, residence, date of muster, and remarks) from California, Connecticut, Georgia, Illinois, Indiana, Iowa, Kansas, Kentucky, Maine, Maryland, Massachusetts, Michigan, Nebraska, New Hampshire, New York, North Carolina, Ohio, Pennsylvania, Rhode Island, South Carolina, Tennessee, Vermont, and Wisconsin
★   Spanish War and Philippine Insurrection published records and rosters

The East Research Room

The pensions and compiled service records files are delivered to this room. There are also two copiers in the room, one of which serves as a bulk copier.

Bulk copy machines allow researchers to make copies for one hour at a time. Appointments are made at the reference desk in Room 203. Only one-hour appointments can be made at a time. People working as a team are one person for purposes of using the bulk copier. As soon as you finish your appointment, you can sign up for another one. A microfilm-to-paper bulk copier is available for half-hour appointments in Room 400.

FEDERAL CENSUS RECORDS

Beginning in 1790, a census has been taken in the United States every ten years. The 1790 through 1920 census schedules are available to the public in Room 400 of the National Archives. The 1930 through 1990 schedules are protected by the Privacy Act and are restricted for seventy-two years from the date they were taken.

Information from these latter schedules may be obtained for a fee if permission of the living person is granted or if the requestor is a blood relative of the deceased person shown on the census. In the latter case, you must submit proof of death of the person listed in the census. For further information and Form BC-600, contact Bureau of the Census, P.O. Box 1545, Jeffersonville, IN 47131.

Original Census Volumes

The original census volumes for pre-1880 census records can be viewed only if the microfilm is illegible.

If you cannot read the microfilm copy, consult a staff member who will verify that the film is illegible and will give you an authorization to request the original census volume. Take this authorization form to Room 203. Obtain the proper volume number for the census from the Special List. It will take about an hour for the volume to be pulled.

Census Schedules

The 1790 through 1840 census records, or schedules, list only the head of the household by name. Other family members are noted by sex in various age categories. The 1850 through 1920 census records list every person in the household by name. Surnames on a page of the schedules are usually arranged in the order in which the enumerator visited each household. A few of the pre-1850 schedules were recopied, and the names are in alphabetical order. While this makes searching easier, the neighborhoods are no longer preserved intact.

Many of the census records are indexed. There are book indexes for all of the 1790 to 1850 records and for many of the 1860 and 1870 records in the Finding Aids Room (Room 402). The index system for the 1880, 1900, and 1910 records is called the Soundex or Miracode.

The Soundex Coding System

The soundex is an index to the census that groups together names which contain similar sounds but which are not necessarily spelled or pronounced the same. Therefore, you will find the names Byrne, Brown, Byrum, and Barron filed together.

To use the soundex a surname is converted into a four-place code consisting of the first letter of the surname followed by three numbers. For example, the soundex code for Brown is B650. The numbers are assigned according to the following guide:

Soundex Coding Guide

The number	represents the letters
1	B P F V
2	C S K G J Q X Z
3	D T
4	L
5	M N
6	R

➤ The letters A E I O U W Y H are not coded.
➤ The first letter of a surname is not coded.
➤ Every soundex number must be three digits.
➤ If there are not three digits, complete with zeros.
➤ Disregard double letters in the name. Code names with a prefix both ways.
➤ Mac, Mc, O, etc., are not considered prefixes.
➤ Disregard letters with the same code number.

Using the Soundex

The soundex consists of individual index cards. All cards with the same soundex code are grouped together and filed alphabetically by first name.

Find the code on the soundex film. The codes are in numerical order. Within that code, find the given name of the person. First names are filed alphabetically. Within the same code and same first name, cards are filed in order by county of residence. First names plus middle initials follow listings for first names only.

With both the 1910 miracode and soundex, abbreviations are not interfiled with full spellings. They are listed in strict alphabetical order. Therefore, Wm is found after all William entries, and Jno is found before all John entries.

Information on the Soundex Card

Information given includes the surname, first name, state and county of residence, city, age, place of birth, and whether a U.S. citizen. Each card also lists the volume, enumeration district, sheet number, and line number where the person can be found on the census schedule.

On the soundex microfilm are family cards which are arranged by the name of the head of the household. There are also individual cards for people other than those in the immediate household (husband, wife, son, daughter) who are enumerated with a family. These include grandparents, cousins, boarders, and servants. The card also shows the name of the head of the household or the institution name where the person was living.

Problems with the Soundex

If you have trouble finding a person on the soundex, the following suggestions may be of some help:

➤ Make sure the surname is coded correctly.
➤ Check for an alternate spelling of the surname that would produce a different code.
➤ Within the code be sure to check all possible name combinations, including initials only, nicknames, and reversal of first and middle names.
➤ Check for a misspelled name. Jaems will be alphabetically separate from James.
➤ Both the indexes and the records themselves are subject to error.
➤ The person may have been missed by the indexer or the census taker.
➤ The soundex card may have been filmed out of order.
➤ The name may have been badly misspelled, or the name may have been coded improperly.

Enumeration Districts (ED)

Census schedules are arranged by state or territory, and then by county, and beginning in 1880 by ED. EDs were the areas that an enumerator covered in taking the census. To consult the schedules for a particular town, a minor civil division or geographical area, or a ward of a large city, one must know the enumeration district.

Working with the Census Records

➤ Work from the known to the unknown. Start at the present and work back in time.

➤ Use the *Federal Population Censuses, 1790–1890,* the *1900 Federal Population Census,* the *1910 Federal Population Census,* and the *1920 Federal Population Census* catalogs to identify the number of the film to be examined.

➤ Go to the metal storage drawers that are marked with the census year and state.

➤ Use the assigned reader. Operating instructions are on each machine.

➤ Copy all identifying numbers (i.e., roll number, page number, enumeration district number) so that you will have a complete record of the specific source of the information.

➤ Keep a record of what you have searched. Record each search you make to avoid duplicating the effort later.

➤ Use all indexes with caution. An index is only as good as the indexer. Errors exist in these indexes. If you know that a person was in a certain area at the time of a census but he does not appear in the index, make a page-by-page search for him. He may have been missed in the index. However, before undertaking such a search, make sure you have checked the index for him under all alternate and phonetic spellings.

➤ Do not confuse the soundex indexes with the census films. The soundex films are small (16mm); the census films are large (35mm).

➤ The microfilm may also show code numbers or letters in some of the columns. The codes usually represent household composition, occupation and class of worker, or simply marks made in the coding, punching, or tabulating operations themselves, and should be ignored.

__Fourteenth Census of the U.S., 1920__ (T625), 2,076 rolls

The original 1920 census schedules no longer exist. They have been reproduced on microfilm from master negatives furnished by the Bureau of the Census. The original film includes defects that affect the legibility of some frames.

On 1 January 1920, the Bureau of the Census began taking the fourteenth census of the United States. The Department of Agriculture had requested that the date be changed from the traditional spring/early summer dates to January. The department argued that harvests would be completed and information about the harvests fresh in farmers' minds, and more people would be home in January than in April.

The 1920 census schedules are arranged by state or territory, and thereunder by county, and finally by enumeration district. The states are arranged alphabetically; however, Alaska, Guam and American Samoa, Hawaii, military and naval schedules, the Panama Canal, Puerto Rico, and the Virgin Islands (taken in 1917) are listed last. There was no separate Indian schedule for 1920.

The format and information in the 1920 census schedules closely resemble that of the 1910 census. The 1920 census, however, did not ask about unemployment on the day of the census, nor did it ask about service in the Union or Confederate army or navy. Questions about the number of children born and how long a couple had been married were also omitted. The Bureau modified the enumeration of inmates of institutions and dependent, defective, and delinquent cases. The 1920 census included four new questions, one asking the year of naturalization and three asking about mother tongue.

Because of the changes in some boundaries following World War I, enumerators were instructed to report the province (state or region) or city of persons declaring they or their parents had been born in Austria-Hungary, Germany, Russia, or Turkey. If a person had been born in any other foreign country, only the name of the country was to be entered.

The instructions to the enumerators did not require that individuals spell out their names. Enumerators wrote down the information given to them; they were not authorized to request proof of age, date of arrival, or other information. People were known to change their ages between censuses and some people claimed not to know their age. The race determination was based on the enumerator's impressions.

Individuals were enumerated as residents of the place in which they regularly slept, not where they worked or might be visiting. People with no regular residence, including "floaters" and members of transient railroad or construction camps, were enumerated as residents of the place where they were when the enumeration was taken. Enumerators were also asked if any family members were temporarily absent; if so, these were to be listed either with the household *or* on the last schedule for the census subdivision. Thus, the user should always check that page.

1920 Indexes
The 1920 soundex films (T230) are available for all states. There are two separate soundex cards for the 1920 census, the "family card" and the "individual card." The family card is arranged by the name of the head of the household.

The individual card gives the names of people other than those of the immediate household (husband, wife, son, daughter) who are enumerated with a family. These include grandparents, cousins, boarders, and servants. The card also shows the name of the head of this household or the institution name where the person was living.

Thirteenth Census of the U.S., 1910 (T624), 1,784 rolls

1910 Indexes T1259 to T1279
Available for twenty-one states: Alabama, Arkansas, California, Florida, Georgia, Illinois, Kansas, Louisiana, Michigan, Mississippi, Missouri, North Carolina, Ohio, Kentucky, Oklahoma, Pennsylvania, South Carolina, Tennessee, Texas, Virginia, and West Virginia.

For those states with no index, a page-by-page search must be made to find the family. The closer you can pinpoint where the family was living in 1910, the shorter will be your search. If the family lived in a large city, a city directory can be used to obtain an address.

For some cities there is an ED index. Each city is indexed by street and house number. This index is on microfiche and is available in Room 400 at the National Archives.

Using an ED Index

➤ Consult the three-page list of cities indexed. Across from each city will be the microfiche number on which that city appears.
➤ Put the proper microfiche in the reader and locate the address on the index. Opposite it you will find an ED number. Copy this number.
➤ Check *The 1910 Federal Population Census* booklet for the number of the film containing the ED you want. Look first for the state, then for the county, and then for the ED number.
➤ Put the microfilm on the reader and turn to the ED you obtained from the microfiche. Do a page-by-page search of this ED for the address. The street name will be written sideways on the left of the schedule.
➤ If you do not find the address in the indicated ED, search the EDs before and after it.

The following cities have ED indexes:

Akron, OH	New York City, NY
Atlanta, GA	Brooklyn
Baltimore, MD	Bronx
Canton, OH	Manhattan
Charlotte, NC	Richmond
Chicago, IL	Oklahoma City, OK
Cleveland, OH	Omaha, NE
Dayton, OH	Paterson, NJ
Denver, CO	Peoria, IL
Detroit, MI	Philadelphia, PA
Elizabeth, NJ	Phoenix, AZ
Erie, PA	Reading, PA
Fort Wayne, IN	Richmond, VA
Gary, IN	San Antonio, TX
Grand Rapids, MI	San Diego, CA
Indianapolis, IN	San Francisco, CA
Kansas City, KS	Seattle, WA
Long Beach, CA	South Bend, IN
Los Angeles, CA	Tampa, FL
Newark, NJ	Tulsa, OK

Washington, DC
Wichita, KS
Youngstown, OH

In addition to the microfiche ED index, there is a printed index of three volumes for Nebraska:

★ *Guide to the 1910 Census EDs in Nebraska*

★ *Street Guide to the 1910 Census of Lincoln*

★ *Street Guide to the 1910 Census of Omaha*

Twelfth Census of the U.S., 1900 (T623), 1,854 rolls

The 1900 soundex films (T1030 to T1083) are available for all states.

Eleventh Census of the U.S., 1890 (M407), 3 rolls

More than 99 percent of this census was destroyed by fire in 1921, leaving only fragments containing 6,160 names over limited areas in Alabama, the District of Columbia, Georgia, Illinois, Minnesota, New Jersey, New York, North Carolina, Ohio, South Carolina, Texas.

The 1890 index, M496, 2 rolls, is an alphabetical index for the few surviving 1890 population schedules.

Schedules Enumerating Union Veterans and Widows . . . Civil War, 1890 (M123), 118 rolls.

Special schedules of the 1890 census, enumerating Civil War Union veterans and widows of Union veterans, are available on microfilm for the District of Columbia, half of Kentucky, and alphabetically from Louisiana to Wyoming. There is no microfilmed index to the special 1890 census. The schedules are arranged by state, then by county, and then by township. A page-by-page search must be made.

Information on Veterans' Schedules

✓ Name of veteran (or names of widow and veteran)
✓ Veteran's rank, company, regiment, or vessel
✓ Date of enlistment
✓ Date of discharge
✓ Length of service
✓ Post office and address of each person listed
✓ Disability incurred by the veteran

1885 Census

The states of Colorado, Florida, and Nebraska and the territories of New Mexico and Dakota elected to take an 1885 census with federal assistance. The unbound population, agriculture, and mortality schedules have been microfilmed. The microfilm rolls are available in Room 400. The agriculture schedules are combined on the same rolls with the population schedules. Use the individual descriptive pamphlets for the following microfilm publication numbers to determine which roll number you need.

There is no index for the 1885 census. A page-by-page search must be made.

★ Colorado (M158), 8 rolls
★ Florida (M845), 13 rolls
★ Nebraska (M352), 56 rolls
★ New Mexico (M846), 6 rolls
★ South Dakota (GR27), 3 rolls

**Tenth Census of the U.S., 1880** (T9), 1,454 rolls

Information on Schedules

✓   Place of residence
✓   Name of each person in household
✓   Relationship of each person to head
       of household
✓   Age (month if born within the year)
✓   Sex, color (white, black, mulatto,
       Chinese, Indian)
✓   Marital status
✓   If married within the year
✓   Occupation and months unemployed
✓   Place of birth
✓   Places of birth of parents
✓   School attendance
✓   If able to read and write
✓   If sick or disabled

1880 Indexes
The 1880 soundex films (T734 to T780) are
available for all states but list only those house-
holds with a child ten years of age or younger.
Within the same code and same name, the cards
have been filmed in order by place of birth.

**Ninth Census of the U.S., 1870** (M593), 1,748
rolls

Information on Schedules

✓   Place of residence
✓   Name of each person in household
✓   Age
✓   Sex, color (white, black, mulatto,
       Chinese, Indian)
✓   Place of birth
✓   Value of real estate; value of personal
       property
✓   Occupation
✓   If parents foreign born
✓   If born within the year (month is
       given)
✓   If married within the year (month is
       given)
✓   If attended school
✓   If able to read and write
✓   If deaf-mute, blind, insane, or idiotic
✓   If male citizen of U.S. over twenty-
       one

There are only book indexes by state for the
1870 census. Not all states have been indexed.

**Eighth Census of the U.S., 1860** (M653), 1,438
rolls

Information on Schedules

✓   Name of each person in household
✓   Age, sex, color (white, black,
       mulatto)
✓   Occupation of persons over fifteen
✓   Value of real estate; value of personal
       property
✓   Place of birth
✓   If married within the year
✓   If attended school within the year
✓   If able to read and write
✓   If deaf-mute, blind, insane, an idiot, a
       pauper, or a convict

There are only book indexes by state to the
1860 census. Not all states have been indexed.

Colorado is indexed with Kansas, Montana with
Nebraska, Nevada with Utah, Oklahoma with
Arkansas, and Wyoming with Nebraska.

1860 Census, Slave Schedules in M653
A page-by-page search must be made. There
are no indexes. Information on schedules:

✓   Name and place of residence of slave
       owner
✓   Age, sex, color of slave
✓   Whether slave is a deaf-mute, blind,
       insane, or an idiot
✓   Whether slave is a fugitive from the
       state; name of slave is not given

**Seventh Census of the U.S., 1850** (M432),
1,009 rolls

Information on Schedules

✓   Place of residence
✓   Name of each person in household
✓   Age, sex, color (white, black,
       mulatto)
✓   Occupation

✓ Value of real estate
✓ Place of birth
✓ If married within the year
✓ If attended school within the year
✓ If unable to read or write for persons over twenty
✓ If a pauper or convict
✓ If deaf-mute, blind, insane, or an idiot

Book Indexes are available for all states.

1850 Census, Slave Schedules in M432
A page-by-page search must be made. There are no indexes. Information on schedules is the same as that given in the 1860 schedules.

Sixth Census of the U.S., 1840 (M704), 580 rolls, and ***Fifth Census of the U.S., 1830*** (M19), 201 rolls

Information on Schedules

✓ Name of head of household
✓ Place of residence
✓ Number of free white males/females
Age 0/5
Age 5/10
Age 10/15
Age 15/20
Age 20/30
Age 30/40
Age 40/50
Age 50/60
Age 60/70
Age 70/80
Age 80/90
Age 90/100
Age 100+
✓ Number of male/female slaves and free colored persons
Age 0/10
Age 10/24
Age 24/36
Age 36/55
Age 55/100
Age 100+
✓ Number of persons employed in each of seven classes of occupations

1840 Indexes
There are book indexes for Alabama, Arkansas, Connecticut, Delaware, the District of Co-lumbia, Florida, Georgia, Illinois, Indiana, Iowa, Kentucky, Louisiana, Maine, Maryland, Massachusetts, Michigan, Mississippi, Missouri, New Hampshire, New Jersey, New York, North Carolina, Ohio, Pennsylvania, Rhode Island, South Carolina, Tennessee, Texas, Vermont, Virginia, and Wisconsin.

1830 Indexes
There are book indexes for the same states as 1840 with the exception of Iowa and Louisiana.

Fourth Census of the U.S., 1820 (M33), 142 rolls, and ***Third Census of the U.S., 1810*** (M252), 71 rolls

Information on Schedules

✓ Name of head of household and place of residence
✓ Number of free white males/females
Age 0/10
Age 10/16
Age 16/26
Age 26/45
Age 45+
✓ All other free persons, except Indians not taxed
✓ Number of slaves

1820 schedules for Washington County, Ohio are filmed separately in M1803.

1820 Indexes
There are book indexes for Alabama, Connecticut, Delaware, the District of Columbia, Georgia, Illinois, Indiana, Kentucky, Louisiana, Maine, Maryland, Massachusetts, Mississippi, New Hampshire, New York, North Carolina, Ohio, Pennsylvania, Rhode Island, South Carolina, Tennessee, Texas, Vermont, and Virginia.

1810 Indexes
There are book indexes for Connecticut, Delaware, the District of Columbia, Illinois, Kentucky, Louisiana, Maine, Maryland, Massachusetts, New Hampshire, New York, North Carolina, Pennsylvania, Rhode Island, South Carolina, Vermont, and Virginia.

Second Census of the U.S., 1800 (M32), 52 rolls

Information on Schedules

- ✓ Name of head of household and place of residence
- ✓ Number of free white males/females
  Age   0/10   [born 1790–1800]
  Age 10/16   [born 1784–1790]
  Age 16/26   [born 1774–1784]
  Age 26/45   [born 1745–1774]
  Age 45+   [born pre–1745]
- ✓ All other free persons, except Indians not taxed
- ✓ Number of slaves

1800 schedules for Washington County, territory northwest of the Ohio River, are filmed separately in M1804.

1800 Indexes

There are book indexes for Connecticut, Delaware, the District of Columbia, Kentucky, Maine, Maryland, Massachusetts, New Hampshire, New York, North Carolina, Pennsylvania, Rhode Island, South Carolina, and Vermont.

First Census of the U.S., 1790 (M637), 12 rolls

No schedules are known to exist for Delaware, Georgia, Kentucky, New Jersey, Tennessee, and Virginia. The Virginia schedules were reconstructed from state enumerations. Other schedules were reconstructed from tax records.

Information on Schedules

- ✓ Name of head of household and place of residence
- ✓ Number of free white males over sixteen
- ✓ Number of free white males under sixteen
- ✓ Number of free white females
- ✓ All other free persons
- ✓ Number of slaves

1790 Indexes

There are book indexes for Connecticut, Delaware, Georgia, Kentucky, Maine, Maryland, Maine, New Hampshire, New York, North

Carolina, Pennsylvania, Rhode Island, South Carolina, Vermont, and Virginia.

Nonpopulation Census Schedules

Nonpopulation schedules are those records that contain information on mortality, agriculture, manufacturing, and social statistics. Although they are frequently overlooked by researchers, these schedules can be checked for information about the community in which an ancestor lived. Agricultural and manufacturing schedules are valuable for researching ancestors in rural areas, as farmers often ran associated manufacturing businesses, such as tanning, grain and lumber milling, coopering, brewing, wine making, etc.

Mortality Schedules

A mortality schedule is a list made at the time a census was taken of those persons who died during the preceding year. Although the information given varies for the different census years, all schedules contain the following information:

- ✓ Name of deceased
- ✓ Age, sex, color
- ✓ Marital status
- ✓ Place of birth
- ✓ Occupation
- ✓ Month and cause of death
- ✓ Length of final illness

These schedules can be especially helpful in determining deaths that occurred before state and county records were kept. Mortality schedules may be the only record of death when gravestone or cemetery records do not exist. They are of particular value in searching for records of children for whom no other documentation exists. Room 400 has many of the 1850–1885 mortality schedules. Check the *1972 Census Information* booklet in Room 400 for schedules available in the Archives. Schedules not available at the Archives can usually be found in the various states.

Agriculture Schedules

There are agriculture schedules for 1850, 1860, 1870, 1880, and 1885, some of which are in the National Archives. Check the *1972 Census Information* booklet in Room 400 to determine which schedules are in the Archives.

Every farm of a certain acreage and annual production was enumerated. Although the schedules vary from census year to census year, all schedules contain the following information:

✓   Name of owner, agent, or tenant
✓   Kind/value of acreage
✓   Kind/value of machinery
✓   Kind/value of livestock
✓   Kind/value of produce

Industry / Manufacturers Schedules

There are industrial schedules for 1810, 1820, 1850, 1860, 1870, 1880, and 1885, some of which are at the NARA. Check the *1972 Census Information* booklet in Room 400 for the schedules available.

The information varies from census year to census year. In general, all schedules contain information about manufacturing, mining, and fisheries. All schedules contain the following information:

✓   Type of business or product
✓   Amount of capital invested
✓   Quantities, kinds, and value of raw materials used
✓   Quantities, kinds, and value of product produced annually
✓   Kind of power or machinery used
✓   Number of men and women employed
✓   Average monthly cost of labor

EXAMPLE: Isaac Stiles operated a lumber business in Greene County, Ohio. The 1870 industry schedule for Spring Valley Township, Greene County, Ohio gives the following information about Isaac's business:

✓   Stiles, Isaac
✓   Business: lumber sawed
✓   Invested: $2,000
✓   Motive power: water/16 horsepower
✓   Machines: 5 saws
✓   Avg # hands employed: 1

✓   Amt pd in wages for yr: $150
✓   Months in active operation: 8
✓   Materials: 133,000 feet of logs; value: $1,330
✓   Production: 1,000,000 feet/lumber; value: $2,000 and 15 cords of wood, value: $45

Enumeration District Descriptive Rolls

These rolls contain descriptions of the geographic subdivisions used in taking the U.S. census from 1830 to 1950. An enumeration district is an area of such size that could be covered by a single census taker within one census period. This area could be as large as a county or as small as part of a city block. The 1930 through 1990 censuses are not available for searching.

The 1880, 1900, 1910, and 1920 descriptive rolls are of the most value. They can be used in conjunction with the 1880, 1900, 1910, and 1920 ED maps or a good city street map to locate a specific address, which can be found from a city directory.

Obtain an address for your ancestor from an appropriate city directory during the proper time period.

If there is an ED map for the place and census year you want, find your address on it and make a note of the ED into which it falls. Preliminary Inventory Number 103, *Cartographic Records of the Bureau of the Census,* lists ED maps available for each state from 1880 to 1940.

To view an ED map, you must go to Archives II. Another alternative is to locate your address on a good city street map, making note of the nearby cross streets. Check the proper year for the ED descriptive roll and match up the ED description with the area in which your address appears. You may come up with three or four possible EDs if the ED boundaries happen to be the street on which your address is located.

Once you have determined the EDs in which you are interested, do a page-by-page search for the address. The street is written sideways at the far left side of the schedule. The house number is written in the first column on the left.

MILITARY RECORDS

All directions and microfilm publication numbers (in parentheses) refer to films in Room 400 and original records in Room 203.

Military personnel records for the following wars are in Archives I:

War	Approximate Dates
American Revolution	1775–1783
War of 1812	1812–1815
Mexican War	1846–1848
Civil War	1861–1865
Spanish American War	1898–1901
Philippine Insurrection	1899–1902
Various Indian wars	1784–1890s

Pension Records

Over the years pensions have been awarded to veterans and to widows or heirs of veterans. Although pension files vary in the amount of data they contain, as a rule they are rich in genealogical information. The Civil War pensions will usually contain more family information than the Revolutionary War or War of 1812 pension files. A widow's pension file will usually contain more family information than a veteran's file. The following items may be found in a pension file:

✓ Date and place of birth of soldier
✓ Date and place of death of soldier
✓ Marriage of soldier, including previous marriages
✓ Birth records of soldier's children
✓ Birth and death dates of soldier's widow
✓ Divorce records
✓ Family Bible records
✓ Dates of military service, where/at what age enlisted
✓ Illnesses/injuries of the soldier
✓ Places of residence since soldier left service
✓ Physical description of the soldier
✓ Affidavits of family, friends, neighbors, etc.

Some pension records have been microfilmed; others must be examined in the original.

Revolutionary War Pension and Bounty Land Warrant Application Files (M804), 2,670 rolls

The records are arranged alphabetically. Be sure to check for all spellings of a name. For quick reference, use Virgil White's *Genealogical Abstracts of Revolutionary War Pension Files* (Waynesboro, TN: National Historical Publishing Co., 1990–1992).

Each file begins with an identification card containing the veteran's name, his widow's name (if a widow's pension), the state from which the veteran served, and the pension number. Following this card are the documents, which are usually divided into "selected" and "non-selected" sections.

When the records were filmed, the more genealogically significant documents were placed in the selected section, with the remainder of the documents going in the non-selected section. Always research the non-selected records as well as the selected records. The selection process is subject to error, and you may find a very important document buried in the non-selected section.

Some file identification cards are marked with a star denoting the file contains ten pages or less and is not divided into selected and non-selected sections. When ordering pension records through the mail, the star marking indicates whether you have an entire file or just the selected documents. If the identification card contains a star, you have the entire file. If the identification card contains no star, you have only the selected documents.

If a pension file contains no death date for the pensioner, check the Final Payment Ledgers. These ledgers sometimes contain the pensioner's date of death. When they do not, a date of death can be approximated from the last quarter the pensioner was paid.

Procedure for Obtaining Final Payment Voucher Information

Make a note of the following information from the beginning of the pension file:

✓　Name
✓　Pension agency
✓　Pension act
✓　File number
✓　Certificate number

Locate the book called *Key to Final Pension Payments Revolutionary War*. This key is arranged alphabetically by state and then by agency and pension act number. Across from the state, agency, and act number are volume and page numbers. Copy these. Consult the key in the front of the notebook. Write down the roll number, which is across from the volume number.

Locate the *Ledgers of Payments to U.S. Pensioners* (T718), 23 rolls. Select the roll number.

When you have the film, turn to the page numbers you noted earlier. The pensioners will be arranged alphabetically by first letter of the surname within each state division. Find the pensioner and copy the death date, if given, and the quarter of last payment.

If the pensioner's date of death is shown in the pension payment volume, his heirs may be named in the final payment voucher. To see the original record, fill out NA Form 14001, listing the following:

✓　Final payment voucher, Revolutionary War
✓　Name
✓　Pension agency
✓　Pension act
✓　File number
✓　Certificate number
✓　Death date

Submit all requests for copies of final payment vouchers. If the pensioner's date of death is not shown in the pension payment volume, it usually means that heirs are not named in the payment voucher. You may, of course, still look at the original documents if you wish. Fill out NA Form 14001 and take it to the Service Desk.

Old War, War of 1812, Indian Wars, Mexican War Pensions

Indexes
The following indexes are available:

★　*Old War Index to Pension Files 1815–1926* (T316), 7 rolls
★　*Index to War of 1812 Pension Application Files* (M313), 102 rolls
★　*Index to Indian Wars Pension Files, 1892–1926* (T318), 12 rolls
★　*Index to Mexican War Pension Files, 1887–1926* (T317), 14 rolls

Copy the following information, if given, from the alphabetical indexes:

✓　Name of veteran
✓　Name of his widow or other dependent
✓　Service unit
✓　Pension application number
✓　Pension certificate number
✓　Bounty land warrant application number
✓　State from which claim was made

Records
The pension records have not been microfilmed. Fill out and submit NA Form 14027 in Room 400.

The Civil War and Later Pensions

Index
The *General Index to Pension Files, 1861–1934* (T288), 544 rolls, is available on microfilm in Room 400. Copy all of the following information from the alphabetical index, including any C or XC number at the bottom of the index card.

✓　Name of the veteran
✓　Name of his widow or other dependent
✓　Service data
✓　Application number
✓　Date of application

✓   Certificate number
✓   State from which claim was made

Records
The pension records have not been microfilmed. Fill out and submit NA Form 14027 in Room 400. If they are filed in the Archives, the records will be available for viewing in Room 203. Only pensions awarded by the U.S. government will be found at the Archives. Confederate pensions were awarded by the individual southern states and will be found in the archives of the state which awarded the pension.

The C and XC numbers indicate pensions that either are or were in the possession of the Veterans Administration. Some C and XC numbered pensions were returned to the Archives; others are still at the Department of Veterans Affairs.

The following numbered files will not be at the Archives:

✓   Any six digit number
✓   Any number before 2,200,000
✓   Any number after 3,001,000

There are exceptions to the above. Always check with the Archives first for any C or XC number.

If NA Form 14027 is returned with "Not at Archives" checked, you will have to contact the Department of Veterans Affairs to make arrangements to view the pension.

Organization Index to Pension Files of Veterans Who Served Between 1861 and 1900 (T289), 765 rolls
This index is arranged alphabetically by state, then by branch of service, then numerically by regiment, then alphabetically by company, and lastly alphabetically by the veteran's surname.

Bounty Land Warrants

Bounty land warrants were granted to certain veterans, or their heirs, on the basis of service rendered to the U.S. between 1775 and 1855. A bounty land warrant gave the warrantee a right to free land in the public domain.

All warrants were assignable, except for War of 1812 warrants used before 1852. The claimant could either locate his warrant, i.e., exchange the warrant for land in the public domain, or sell it. Most recipients of bounty land warrants chose to sell them. There are two kinds of records for research: the applications and the surrendered warrants. They are found in two record groups:

★   *Records of the Veterans Administration*, RG 15
★   *Records of the Bureau of Land Management*, RG 49

Bounty Land Warrant Application Files
A claimant submitted an application for a bounty land warrant with affidavits of witnesses, marriage records, and other evidence of identity and service. Therefore, the application files contain much the same information as the pension files. Bounty land application files are accessed as follows:

★   Revolutionary War Bounty Land Warrants. Bounty land warrant applications are interfiled with pensions in *Revolutionary War Pension and Bounty Land Warrant Application Files* (M804), 2,670 rolls. Sometimes there is only an index card for the bounty land. Over 14,000 application files were destroyed by fire in 1800.

★   War of 1812 Bounty Land Warrants Some bounty land warrant applications are listed in the *Index to War of 1812 Pension Application Files* (M313), 102 rolls. This index is on microfilm in Room 400.

★   Unindexed Warrants Dated Through 1855. If the veteran is not listed in the above indexes, fill out Form 14027 and request an unindexed bounty land search. You must have the name of the soldier, the name of his unit, the state from which he served, and the war in which he served. If you do not know this information, you will have to consult the appropriate service record index.

Submit the form in Room 400. The records will be available for viewing in Room 203 in about an hour and a half.

★ <u>Surrendered Bounty Land Warrants,</u> RG 49. The files identify the patentee by name and usually indicate where and when the tract of land was acquired. The original files are maintained at Archives I. The patents are maintained by the Bureau of Land Management, Eastern States (BLM-ES) in Springfield, VA.

The types of bounty land warrants are as follows:

U.S. Revolutionary War Bounty Land Warrants Used in the U.S. Military District of Ohio . . . (M829), 16 rolls

The warrants, related papers, registers, and indexes have been microfilmed. If you know the soldier's name, use the pension indexes. If you have only the warrant number, use the indexes on M829.

The first series of warrants, based on an ordinance of 1788, records only the following information:

✓ Name of veteran
✓ Date of issue of warrant
✓ Name of heir/assignee

The second series of warrants, based on a legislative act of 1803, records the legal description of the land in addition to the information from the first series.

Virginia Revolutionary War Warrants Surrendered for Land in the U. S. Military District of Ohio, RG 49

These warrants were based on service in the Continental Line of Virginia and were originally issued for Kentucky land south of the Green River. Later, the warrants could be surrendered for land in the U.S. Military District of Ohio. A complete file includes the following:

✓ Surrendered warrant
✓ Certification of location
✓ Survey
✓ Power of attorney
✓ Assignment
✓ Affidavit concerning heirs of veteran

The application files are in the Virginia State Library, Richmond, VA. The surrendered warrant files are at Archives I. To access these records you need the volume and page numbers that identify the case file. There are three finding aids in Room 400 that will help you:

★ Index to "The Names of Warrantees" is arranged alphabetically. Obtain the warrant number.

★ Register of "Virginia Military Warrants, Numerical, Continental and State Lines" is arranged by warrant numbers. Obtain the survey number.

★ Register of "Surveys for Land on Virginia Military District, Ohio" is arranged by survey numbers. Obtain the volume and page numbers that identify the case file.

Revolutionary War Warrants Surrendered for Scrip Certificates (M829), 16 rolls
After 1830 Revolutionary War warrants could be surrendered for scrip certificates. Warrants could be exchanged only for land within certain geographical areas. Scrip certificates, on the other hand, could be exchanged for any available land in the public domain. A complete file includes the following:

✓ Name of veteran
✓ Names and relationships of heirs
✓ Places of residence
✓ Date of surrender of warrant

There is an alphabetical index to the U.S. Warrants Surrendered 1830–1881 and the Virginia Warrants Surrendered 1830–1847. There is also an index to the Virginia Warrants Surrendered 1852–1897.

War of 1812 Military Bounty Land Warrants, 1815–1858 (M848), 14 rolls
The bounty land districts were in Arkansas, Il-

linois, and Missouri. Until 1842 the warrants had to be used within these districts, and until 1852 they were unassignable, except by inheritance. A complete file includes the following:

✓   Name of warrantee
✓   Legal description of land
✓   Date of patent

The warrants and the index to the warrants have been microfilmed and are available in Room 400. If you know the soldier's name, use the pension indexes. If you have only the warrant number, use the indexes on M848.

U.S. Warrants Issued for Unspecified Lands
These warrants are primarily dated 1847 to 1859. A complete file includes the following:

✓   Name of warrantee
✓   Date of patent
✓   Legal description of land

To access these warrants you must have the complete warrant number. These warrants are filed by date of act, then by number of acres, and then by warrant number. Obtain the warrant number from an unindexed bounty land search at the National Archives.

Volunteer Service Records

When there were not enough enlistments in the regular army and militia, men were conscripted to serve in non-regular or volunteer military units. To access these records, you need to know the serviceman's full name, approximate years of service (or the war in which he served), and state from which he served. Copies of service records can be made from the microfilm or the original documents.

The following information may be found in a service record:

✓   Name and rank
✓   Military unit
✓   Dates of entry into service, discharge, or separation by desertion, dismissal, or death
✓   Age and place of birth (the latter is rare except for Spanish-American War records)
✓   Residence at time of enlistment

If you cannot find the serviceman in a volunteer unit, check the regular Army records for him. Keep in mind also that the serviceman may have served in a state militia unit never mustered into federal service. In this case, there will be no record of him on file in the Archives (check with the state).

It is also possible that the veteran's records were destroyed or his name misspelled. Be sure to check under all possible spellings.

Compiled Service Records of Soldiers . . . American Army During the Revolutionary War (M881), 1,097 rolls

Index
The *General Index to . . . Service Records Revolutionary War Soldiers* (M860), 58 rolls, is on microfilm.

Records
Locate the serviceman in the index and note his unit and state. Consult the *Roll Location Guide* to determine the roll number on which the service records appear. This book is arranged alphabetically by state, then by unit, and thereunder by first letter of surname. Determine which roll of film you need and select it. The records are arranged alphabetically by surname within each unit.

Compiled Service Records of Volunteer Soldiers . . . 1784 to 1811 (M905), 32 rolls

Index
The *Index to 1784 to 1811 Service Records* (M694), 9 rolls, is on microfilm.

Records
When you find the serviceman in the alphabetical index, pull the correct roll of film. The records are arranged alphabetically by surname within each unit.

Requests for Original Military Personnel Records
The 1812 and later pension records and 1812 and later service records, except for Civil War, Confederate, and border state service records, have not been microfilmed, and the original records must be viewed.

Requests for original military, pension, and bounty land records are submitted in Room 400. Use the following procedures to review the original files in Room 203, the Central Research Room.

➢ Obtain a request form and complete one form for each record to be reviewed.
➢ Use a ballpoint pen to complete the four-copy form. Make sure the fourth copy can be read.
➢ Make note of the file information for your own records.
➢ Take the completed form to the Service Desk in Room 400.
➢ Submit your requests for records before 4:00 PM on weekdays.
➢ The original records will be delivered to Room 203 in about one hour.

War of 1812, Mexican War, and Indian Wars Service Records

Indexes
The following indexes are on microfilm and are in Room 400:

★ *Index to Compiled Service Records . . . War of 1812* (M602), 234 rolls
★ *Index to Compiled Service Records . . . Mexican War* (M616), 41 rolls
★ *Index to Compiled Service Records . . . Indian Wars and Disturbances* (M629), 42 rolls

Records
These service records have not been microfilmed. When you find the serviceman in the index, fill out and submit NA Form 14027. In about an hour the records will be available for viewing in Room 203.

Civil War Union Service Records

Indexes
There are only state indexes to Union service records. Therefore, the state from which a person served must be known in order to locate his service record. When you find the serviceman in the index, fill out and submit NA Form 14027. In about an hour and a half the records will be available for viewing in Room 203.

Records
Except for the border states of Missouri, Kentucky, West Virginia, and Maryland, and Union troops raised in the Confederate states, these service records have not been microfilmed. If the man served from one of the border states, you will find his records on microfilm where the films are filed alphabetically by state.

From the index entry, make a note of his unit. Go to the notebooks on top of cabinets and select the one marked "Union" and turn to his state and unit. The film number will be opposite the first letter of the man's surname. The records are arranged alphabetically by surname within each unit.

Civil War Confederate Service Records

Indexes
There is a *Consolidated Index to Compiled Service Records of Confederate Soldiers* (M253), 535 rolls, along with the state Confederate indexes.

Records
These service records have been microfilmed and are available in Room 400. Using either the consolidated index or the appropriate state index, locate the serviceman and make a note of his unit. Go to the notebook marked "Confederate" and look up his state and unit. You will find a film number given opposite the first letter of the man's surname. Select the film from the cabinets which are filed alphabetically by state. The records are arranged alphabetically by surname within each unit.

Spanish American War and Philippine Insurrection Service Records

Index
Use the *General Index to Compiled Service Records . . . War with Spain* (M871), 126 rolls, and/ or, the *Index to Compiled Service Records . . . Philippine Insurrection* (M872), 24 rolls.

Records
These service records have not been microfilmed. When you find the serviceman on the index, fill out and submit NA Form 14027. In about an hour and a half the records will be available for viewing in Room 203.

Regular Army Service Records

Officers

Most personnel-related records of officers are found in the records of the Adjutant General's Office. There are no consolidated files for officers before 1956. Use secondary sources such as the following:

★   *Historical Register of Officers of the Continental Army During the War of the Revolution, April, 1775 to December, 1783,* by Francis Bernard Heitman (Washington, DC: U.S. Government Printing Office, 1914).

★   *The U.S. Army Register* (begins with 1813).

★   *American State Papers.* 38 vols. (Washington, DC: Gales and Seaton, 1832–1861).

Enlisted Men

Most records of enlisted men are found in the records of the Adjutant General's Office, or in the *Registers of Enlistments in the U.S. Army, 1798–1914* (M233), 81 rolls. These registers include the following information:

✓   Name and date of enlistment
✓   Birthplace and age
✓   Occupation
✓   Physical description
✓   Regiment and company
✓   Discharge or death date

Naval and Marine Service Records

Officers

There are two sources to check for abstracts of officers' service records:

★   *Abstracts of Service Records of Naval Officers, 1796–1893* (M330), 19 rolls. Because the entries are chronological, you must know an approximate date of commission.

★   *Abstracts of Service Records of Naval Officers, 1829–1924* (M1328), 18 rolls.

Enlisted Men

Records of Navy enlisted men are dated 1798–1956 and consist of a variety of sources. De-pending upon the time period needed, the following sources should be examined:

★   Ship muster rolls and pay rolls, 1798–1859, 1860–1900, 1898–1939, 1940–1956
★   Registers of enlistments, 1845–1854
★   Weekly returns of enlistments, 1855–1891
★   Quarterly returns of enlistments, 1866–1891
★   Jackets for enlisted men, 1842–1885
★   Continuous service certificates, 1865–1899
★   Personnel record cards, 1901–1917
★   Card abstracts of WWI service records, 1917–1919

To access these records, check with one of the consultants in Room 203.

Office of the Adjutant General

The central files contain records about matters relating to individual servicemen. The Letters Received files contain letters originally received by various War Department offices and divisions and include letters from officers, enlisted men, the President, Congress, private persons, and business firms. The letters deal with a wide variety of subjects, including appointments, discharges, leave, pay, pensions, promotions, recruitments, and transfers of both officers and enlisted personnel.

Registers of Letters Received . . . 1812–1889 (M711), 85 rolls
Indexes to Letters Received . . . 1846, 1861–1889 (M725), 9 rolls
Index to General Correspondence . . . 1890–1917 (M698), 1,269 rolls
Letters Received . . . 1805–1821 (M566), 144 rolls
Letters Received . . . 1822–1860 (M567), 636 rolls
Letters Received . . . 1861–1870 (M619), 828 rolls
Letters Received . . . 1871–1880 (M666), 593 rolls
Letters Received . . . 1881–1889 (M689), 740 rolls

Twentieth-Century Military Records

Military personnel records for the following wars are not available at the National Archives.

War	Approximate Dates
World War I	1917–1918
World War II	1941–1945
Korean War	1950–1953
Vietnam War	1964–1975

Military personnel records for the following services and time periods are not available at the National Archives but can generally be found at the Federal Records Center in St. Louis and are subject to the Privacy Act.

Army	Officers after 1917
	Enlisted after 1912
Air Corps/Air Force	None
Navy	Officers after 1902
	Enlisted after 1895
Marines	Officers after 1902
	Enlisted after 1895
Coast Guard	Officers after 1928
	Enlisted after 1914

To obtain information about a serviceman who served after the above years, fill out Standard Form 180, "Request Pertaining to Military Records," and mail it to the appropriate address indicated on the form. A fire at the Personnel Center in St. Louis in 1973 destroyed many compiled service folders of enlisted men, 1912–1956, and officers, 1917–1956.

There are restrictions on the release of this information. The veteran may have access to almost any information in his own record. If the veteran is deceased, the next of kin is authorized to receive information from a file. The order of precedence of the next of kin is: unremarried widow or widower, eldest child, parent, eldest sibling. Other requesters must have a release authorization signed by the veteran or next of kin.

IMMIGRATION RECORDS

Sources for immigration records at the Archives include:

★ Passenger lists
★ Naturalization records

Passenger Lists

Although there are passenger lists for as early as 1798, primarily baggage lists or cargo manifests, most lists are for the years 1820 to 1945. Passenger arrival lists in the National Archives include records for East Coast, Gulf Coast, Great Lakes, and Pacific Coast ports, and Canadian border crossings, beginning in 1895. Many passenger lists have been microfilmed.

The lists are arranged by port and date of arrival. The *Roll Location Guide* in Room 400 gives the description and location of these records.

Customs Passenger Lists (1820–ca 1883)

The records of the U.S. Customs Service consist of original lists, copies or abstracts, and transcripts. From 1820 the master of a vessel arriving at any U.S. port was required to submit a list of passengers to the collector of customs. This is the *original* list.

The collector of customs was required to submit a quarterly report, or abstract, consisting of copies of passenger lists, to the Secretary of State. Copies and abstracts exist for more ports than do original lists, and generally cover the period 1820 to 1874. These records are *copies* of the original lists.

The Secretary of State was required to submit passenger list information at each session of Congress. During the period 1819 to 1832, the State Department prepared transcripts from the abstracts supplied by the collector of customs. There were originally nine volumes of State Department Transcripts. Volumes one, three, five, eight, and nine, and some entries from volume two, which is missing, are indexed. There are no indexes for volumes three, four, six, and seven. These records are *copies of copies* of the original lists.

IMMIGRANT LABORERS, ca. 1918 (photographed at West New York, NJ)

Information on most Customs Passenger Lists includes the following:

✓ Names of vessel and master
✓ Port of embarkation
✓ Date and port of arrival
✓ Passenger's name, age, sex
✓ Country of residence
✓ Country in which passenger intended to live
✓ Death information, if died en route

Immigration Passenger Lists (ca 1883–1954)

Records of the Immigration and Naturalization Service were maintained by federal immigration officials. Information on most lists includes:

✓ Names of vessel and master
✓ Port of embarkation
✓ Date and port of arrival
✓ Passenger's name, age, sex, marital status
✓ Passenger's occupation and nationality
✓ Passenger's last residence/final destination
✓ Name/address/relationship of person passenger is joining

The post-1907 lists have additional information:

✓ Passenger's personal description
✓ Passenger's place of birth
✓ Name and address of nearest relative in country from which passenger is coming

Indexes

There are name indexes for the passengers arriving at the ports of Baltimore, Boston, New Orleans, New York, and Philadelphia, and miscellaneous ports on the Atlantic and Gulf Coast and on the Great Lakes. The indexes are arranged either alphabetically or according to the soundex system. The indexes consist of cards containing information that leads directly to the passenger lists.

The amount of information on the index cards will vary. On some are found the name, age,

sex, occupation, nationality, last permanent residence, name of vessel, and date of arrival. On others there is only the name, age, sex, and line, page, and volume reference numbers. As some pages have two or three numbers, it is important to remember that the page number given on the index is always the stamped number in the lower left hand corner.

If the index card does not give the name of the ship, it may be necessary to check all the lists contained in the volume number given. To avoid needless searching, check the ship listings at the beginning of the volume. The ships are listed in order of arrival, along with country of origin and number of pages contained in the list. This information can help eliminate certain ship lists.

Book indexes consist of alphabetical listings of passengers provided to the Immigration and Naturalization Service by the shipping lines. They are generally arranged by shipping company, chronologically by ship arrival, and alphabetically by the first letter of the passenger's surname. The lists include the passenger's name, age, and destination.

Quarterly abstracts are consolidated lists of all passengers who arrived at a port during the quarter. They were prepared by the collector of customs and sent to the Secretary of State. They are arranged by port, by quarter, and alphabetically by the first letter of the surname.

Book indexes and quarterly abstracts are useful for making searches when the approximate date of arrival of the immigrant is known. All indexes and abstracts are copies of the original records and as such are subject to copying errors.

The microfilmed records are organized by port of arrival. Indexes are not available for all years. Book indexes are available for Boston, New York, and Philadelphia for selected years.

Baltimore Records

Manifests
- M255   1820–1897
- T844   1891–1909

Indexes
- M326 Index to Passenger Lists of Vessels Arriving at Baltimore, 1833–1866 (City Lists—used to fill in gaps in federal lists)
- M327 Index to Passenger Lists of Vessels Arriving at Baltimore, 1820–1897 (federal lists)
- M334 If the passenger does not appear on the above indexes, check M334 for arrivals prior to 1870.
- T520 Index to Passenger Lists of Vessels Arriving at Baltimore, 1897– July 1952

Quarterly Abstracts
- M596 1820–1869

Boston Records

Manifests
- M277 1820–1891
- T843 1891–1935

Indexes
- M265 Index to Passenger Lists of Vessels Arriving at Boston, 1848–1891
- M334 If the passenger does not appear on the above indexes, check M334 for arrivals prior to 1874.
- T521 Index to Passenger Lists of Vessels Arriving at Boston, 1902–1906
- T617 Index to Passenger Lists of Vessels Arriving at Boston, 1 July 1906– 1920

There is a gap in the indexes between 1891 and 1902.

Book Indexes
- T790 Book Indexes, Boston Passenger Lists, 1899–1940

New Orleans Records

Manifests
- M259 1820–1902
- T905 1903–1945

Indexes
- M334 If you are searching for a pre-1851 arrival, check M334.
- T527 Index to Passenger Lists of Vessels Arriving at New Orleans, 1853– 1899

- T618 Index to Passenger Lists of Vessels Arriving at New Orleans, 1900– 1952

Quarterly Abstracts
- M272 1820–1875

New York Records

Manifests
- M237 1820–17 June 1897
- T715 16 June 1897–1 July 1957

Indexes
- M261 Index to Passenger Lists of Vessels Arriving at New York, 1820–1846
- M1417 Index to Passengers Arriving in New York, 1944–1948
- T519 Index to Passenger Lists of Vessels Arriving at New York, 16 June 1897– 30 June 1902
- T621 Index to Passenger Lists of Vessels Arriving at New York, 1 July 1902– 1943

There is no index for New York from 1847 to 1896. The Balch Institute for Immigration Research at Temple University in Philadelphia has the original manifests for this period and is publishing the indexes in series by ethnic group. Some of these series are:

★ *The Famine Immigrants*, by Ira A. Glazier and Michael Tepper (Baltimore: Genealogical Publishing Co., 1983–).

★ *Germans to America,* by Ira A. Glazier and P. William Filby (Wilmington, DE: Scholarly Resources, 1989–).

★ *Italians to America,* by Ira A. Glazier and P. William Filby (Wilmington, DE: Scholarly Resources, 1992–).

★ *Migration from the Russian Empire,* by Ira A. Glazier (Baltimore: Genealogical Publishing Co., 1995–).

Book Indexes
- T612 1 January 1906–31 December 1942

Philadelphia Records

Manifests
- M425 1800–1882
- T840 1883–1945

Indexes
- M334 If the passenger does not appear on the index below, check M334 for arrivals prior to 1874.
- M360 Index to Passenger Lists of Vessels Arriving in Philadelphia, 1800–1906
- M1500 Records of the Special Boards of Inquiry, District No. 4, Immigration and Naturalization Service (Philadelphia), 1893–1909
- T526 Index to Passenger Lists of Vessels Arriving in Philadelphia, 1883–1948

Book Indexes
- T791 1883–1906

Note: the *Index to Passenger Lists of Vessels Arriving at New York 1902–1943* (T621), 755 rolls, and *Index to Passenger Lists of Vessels Arriving at Philadelphia 1883–1948* (T526), 60 rolls, can be difficult to use because the soundex index cards were reduced in size when they were filmed, and because many cards are faded to the point that they cannot be read. The original cards have been destroyed.

Miscellaneous Ports on the Atlantic and Gulf Coast and on the Great Lakes

Manifests
- T575 1820–1873

Index
- M334 Supplemental Index to Passenger Lists of Vessels Arriving at Atlantic and Gulf Coast Ports (exclusive of New York) 1820–1874. This index is a supplement to the Baltimore, Boston, New Orleans, and Philadelphia indexes.

Published Indexes and Finding Aids

The following publications are located in Room 400 at the National Archives:

Morton Allan Directory of European Passenger Steamship Arrivals. New York steamship arrivals 1890 to 1930 and Baltimore, Boston, Philadelphia arrivals 1904 to 1926 are included. Passengers are not named. The book is organized by year, by steamship company, including port of embarkation, and by a chronological list of ship names and dates of arrival.

Passenger and Immigration Lists Index, 3 vols., by P. William Filby and Mary Meyer (Detroit: Gale Research, 1981), plus supplements. Only lists in print (not original passenger arrival records) are included in this index.

Immigrant and Passenger Arrivals, A Select Catalog of National Archives Microfilm Publications. 2nd ed. (Washington, DC: National Archives Trust Fund Board, 1991).

How to make the most of the information that is known:

➢ *Ship, date, and port known*

The card at the beginning of each roll of microfilm lists the ships given in the roll and indicates how many pages there are for each manifest.

➢ *Port and year known*

Pull the proper index film and search for the immigrant. Once found, make a note of the name of the ship and the line, page, and volume numbers on the index card.

Go to the manifests and pull the film containing the volume number.

Turn to the ship and then look for the page number.

➢ *Year only known*

Check the existing indexes for this period. The scope of this search will be very wide. Before undertaking such a search, make every effort to find a naturalization record, giving the date of arrival in this country.

➢ *Port, ship, and year known*

Check the index first. If there is no record in the index, consult the *Morton Allan Directory* to find the shipping company for the vessel in question. Make a note of ship arrival dates. Pull these passenger lists and search each for the immigrant.

➢ *Port and partial date known*

Check the index first. If there is no record in the index, check the *Morton Allan Directory*.

continued . . .

. . . continued

➤ *Time frame known*

Check all the available filmed indexes to passenger lists first. If the immigrant is not there, chances are that he arrived at the port of New York during the time period that is unindexed.

Consult the Filby and Meyer *Index*, including supplements, and check for the immigrant alphabetically by surname. Each entry contains a reference number and page number. Consult the reference guide in front and back of each volume for the source of the information.

NATURALIZATION RECORDS

Limited naturalization records are available on microfilm in Room 400. The regional archives hold original records of naturalization filed in most of the federal courts located in their regions.

There have been many laws affecting naturalization over the years, and the requirements have varied from a simple oath of allegiance to a seven-year residency. Up until 1922 wives and children under eighteen automatically became citizens when the husband/father did.

The Naturalization Process

The procedure for becoming a naturalized citizen began with a declaration of intent. After the declaration was filed, the immigrant was required to fulfill a residency requirement, which has varied over the years from three to seven years. Once the residency requirement was fulfilled, the immigrant filed his petition to become a citizen, after which he was granted citizenship. The records generated include the following:

✓ Oath of Allegiance
✓ Declaration of Intent (first paper)
✓ Petition for Citizenship (final paper)
✓ Certificate of Naturalization

Depending upon the year, the above records could contain the following information:

✓ name, address, occupation
✓ birthplace, birth date, or age
✓ country, date emigrated
✓ personal description, marital status
✓ last foreign residence
✓ port and date of entry, ship name
✓ time in the U.S.
✓ name/age/address of spouse/children
✓ photograph (after 1940)

Naturalization Prior to 27 September 1906

Prior to 27 September 1906 any court of record (i.e., federal, state, county, or local court) could perform a naturalization. The immigrant usually applied to the court that was closest to him. Depending upon where he lived, this court might not necessarily be in the same county or even the same state as his place of residence. It was not necessary for the declaration of intent to be filed in the same court as the petition for citizenship. Often, the immigrant will have moved during the intervening residency requirement waiting period.

Naturalization after 27 September 1906

After 27 September 1906 naturalizations were performed by the Immigration and Naturalization Service, but federal, district, and state courts continued to perform naturalizations.

Federal Court Naturalization

Naturalizations occurring in a federal court are part of the Records of the District Courts of the United States. A federal court naturalization has declarations containing valuable genealogical information:

Declaration of Intent

✓ name
✓ country of birth/allegiance
✓ date of application
✓ signature
✓ perhaps date of arrival

Applications after 1906 also contain

✓ age, occupation
✓ personal description
✓ date/place of birth
✓ citizenship
✓ present address
✓ last foreign address
✓ vessel/port of embarkation
✓ U.S. port, date of arrival

Naturalization Petition
- ✓ name
- ✓ residence/occupation
- ✓ date/place of birth
- ✓ citizenship
- ✓ personal description
- ✓ date of emigration
- ✓ port of embarkation, arrival
- ✓ marital status
- ✓ name, place of birth, and residence of applicant's children
- ✓ signature

Naturalization Deposition
- ✓ period of the applicant's residence in a given place
- ✓ information about the character of the applicant

Federal naturalization records may be found in the custody of the original court, the appropriate Federal Archives Record Center, or the National Archives. The original naturalization petitions for Maine, Massachusetts, New Hampshire, Rhode Island, and Vermont are located at the Regional Archives in Pittsfield, MA.

Consult NARA publications for availability and location of microfilm records.

Miscellaneous Sources for Naturalization Information

Census records, military pension files, homestead/land grant records, and immigrant passenger lists may contain information about citizenship, naturalization, and country of origin.

Census Records
The 1870 census indicates whether a male over the age of twenty-one was eligible to vote. Since only citizens could vote, this will tell if the immigrant had been naturalized by 1870. The 1900 and 1910 censuses indicate if a man had been naturalized (NA) or had submitted his papers (PA). Until 1922 a woman's citizenship status, if she was married, was dependent upon that of her husband's.

Military Pension Files
A pension file usually contains a list of residences of the soldier, which will give an idea

of where to check for naturalization records. A file may contain an affidavit from a family member, stating when the family came to this country.

Homestead and Federal Land Grant Records
Since only citizens could apply for land, proof of citizenship had to be submitted with the land application. Sometimes this proof is only a sworn statement by the applicant, but there may be an affidavit showing the date and court of naturalization.

PASSPORT RECORDS

The U.S. Passport Office considers a passport to be a "travel document attesting to the citizenship of the bearer." Some 2.6 million passports were issued by this office between 1795 and 1929.

Although passports were not required of U.S. citizens traveling abroad before World War I, except for a short time during the Civil War, they were frequently obtained because of the added protection they afforded.

The National Archives has passport applications from 1791 to 1925 located in Record Groups 59 and 84. Applications less than seventy-five years old may not be used without permission. Although the applications have become more detailed over the years, even the early ones usually contain the following information:

- ✓ Name, age, signature
- ✓ Place of residence
- ✓ Personal description
- ✓ Names or number of persons in family intending to travel
- ✓ Date
- ✓ Date and court of naturalization

They may also contain:
- ✓ Date and place of birth of applicant, spouse, minor children
- ✓ Date, ship, and port of arrival in U.S.

The applications are arranged chronologically; the 1830 to 1925 records are in bound volumes.

The indexes are arranged alphabetically (sometimes by first letter of surname only).

1834–1859	Book Registers
1850–1852	3x5 Card Index
1860–1880	
1881–1905	Book Indexes
1906–1923	3x5 Card Index

Review the index films, M1371, for early passport applications (1810–1906) and for application numbers and date, then ask about access to these records.

NATIVE AMERICAN / INDIAN RECORDS

Many records concerning American Indians who maintained their tribal affiliation are available. Check the National Archives' microfilm catalog *American Indians* for references to microfilmed Indian census records. The best overall reference is Edward E. Hill's *Guide to Records in the National Archives Relating to American Indians* (Washington, DC, 1981). To have unmicrofilmed records brought for your use in the Central Reference Room, see an Archivist in the appropriate reference branch, Monday through Friday, before mid-afternoon.

The records of the central office of the Bureau of Indian Affairs are in the National Archives and include the following: annual census rolls, 1885–1940, applications for enrollment of the Five Civilized Tribes members, annuity payrolls, 1841–1940, Eastern Cherokee claim files, 1902–10.

A recent microfilm publication of the National Archives is the *Schedule of a Special Census of Indians, 1880* (M1791), 5 rolls.

NARA has also published an updated guide to Indian records.

BLACK AND AFRICAN AMERICAN RECORDS

The records that are the most helpful are the following:

★   Census records
★   Military service records
★   Freedman's Bureau records
★   Records containing manumissions, emancipations, and fugitive slave case papers

For more information on NARA records and resources for researching African American genealogy and local history in the District of Columbia, see chapter 9. Room G-9 contains other publications to assist in researching black American records:

★   The *Black Studies* catalog lists records available on microfilm in Room 400.
★   *Preliminary Inventory of the Records of the Bureau of Refugees, Freedmen and Abandoned Lands* (P1174)
★   *List of Free Black Heads of Families in the First Census of the United States, 1790* (SL 34)

CONFEDERATE RECORDS RELATING TO CIVILIANS

Southern Claims Commission and Related Records

Citizens who remained loyal to the Union during the Civil War and who had property seized for use by the U.S. Army could submit a claim to the U.S. Government for reimbursement.

The *Consolidated Index of Claims Reported by the Commission of Claims to the House of Representatives, from 1871 to 1890* (M87), roll 14, is available on microfilm in Room 400, and in book form. For location of the book, see the Textual References Consultant in Room G-7. Consult the index to obtain the name, claim number, state, and county. You need this information to have a file pulled.

Barred or totally disallowed claims are on microfiche in Room 400 of the National Archives. Contact the genealogy staff for location of the approved claims. The records are filed by state and thereunder by county. Records must be requested by 3:00 PM and will be sent to Room 203 for viewing.

The case files for 1871 to 1880 have been published in *Southern Loyalists in the Civil War: The Southern Claims Commission*, by Gary Mills (Baltimore: Genealogical Publishing Co., 1994).

In addition to the Southern Claims Commission records, there are other related records:

✓   *Confederate Papers Relating to Citizens or Business Firms* (M346), 1,158 rolls
✓   Name of individual or firm
✓   Nature of service rendered or goods furnished
✓   *Union Provost Marshals' File of Papers Relating to Individual Civilians* (M345), 300 rolls
✓   Name of citizen who came in contact with the Army
✓   Correspondence
✓   Provost court papers and orders
✓   Passes and transportation permits
✓   Paroles and oaths of allegiance
✓   Claims for compensation for property
✓   *Union Provost Marshals' File of Papers Relating to Two or More Civilians* (M416), 94 rolls

"Amnesty Papers," 1865–1867 (M1003), 73 rolls

The following types of records may be found in a file:

✓   Application for amnesty
✓   Affidavits
✓   Oaths of allegiance
✓   Recommendations for executive clemency
✓   Miscellaneous papers

Most of the applications were submitted by persons from the South, including the states of Alabama, Arkansas, Florida, Georgia, Kentucky, Louisiana, Maryland, Missouri, North Carolina, South Carolina, Tennessee, Texas, Virginia, and West Virginia. Other applications were submitted by persons from the northwest and from persons who designated no residence.

MISCELLANEOUS RECORDS

Tax Records

Internal Revenue Assessment Lists, 1862–1874
These lists show the annual taxes levied on all persons, partnerships, firms, associations, and corporations with an income in excess of $600.00. There are annual, monthly, and special assessment lists in rough alphabetical order that show the following:

✓   names of persons liable for taxation
✓   value of property
✓   amount of tax due

Much of Record Group 58, records of the Internal Revenue Service, has been microfilmed and is available in Room 400.

U.S. Direct Tax of 1798: Tax Lists for . . . Pennsylvania (M372), 24 rolls

In 1798 there was a levy on real property and slaves. The records consist of assessment and collection lists, which are arranged geographically. The index to place names is on the first roll of microfilm.

The Archives only has custody of the Pennsylvania lists. The other surviving lists are in the custody of other repositories:

→   Connecticut Historical Society (Connecticut lists)
→   Historical Society of Delaware (Delaware lists)
→   Maryland Historical Society (District of Columbia and Maryland lists)
→   New England Historic Genealogical Society (Massachusetts, Maine, and New Hampshire lists)
→   Rhode Island Historical Society (Rhode Island lists)

→   Tennessee State Library and Archives
    (Tennessee lists)
→   Vermont Historical Society (Vermont
    lists)

Work Projects Administration, Historical Records Survey, RG 39

These reports were compiled between 1936 and 1943 through an effort to create jobs for unemployed academics and clerical workers.

Basically, the reports were inventories of various state and county records, church archives, and miscellaneous materials. The most well known of the projects are the soundexes for the 1880 and 1910–1920 censuses, and the naturalization petitions for New England and the U.S. District Court for the Eastern District of New York.

Many of the manuscripts were never published. The Archives has copies of most of the published materials. Much of the material has been lost or destroyed, but state depositories still hold a number of manuscripts. For a complete list of what is where, see Loretta L. Hefner's *The WPA Historical Records Survey: A Guide to the Unpublished Inventories, Indexes, and Transcripts* (Chicago: The Society of American Archivists, 1980).

The three main publications at the Archives relating to the WPA are:

★   *Index to Reference Cards for Work Project Administration Project Files, 1935–1937* (T936), 79 rolls
★   *Index to Reference Cards for Work Project Administration Project Files, 1938* (T937), 15 rolls
★   *Index to Reference Cards for Work Project Administration Project Files, 1939–1942* 19 rolls

THE REGIONAL ARCHIVES SYSTEM

National resources in local settings, regional archives are located in or near Anchorage, Atlanta, Boston, Chicago, Denver, Fort Worth, Kansas City, Los Angeles, New York (Manhattan), Philadelphia, Pittsfield (MA), San Francisco, and Seattle. Many of their records are similar and others are unique to a single region.

Research services at each location include textual and microfilm rooms, research assistance on site and by mail and telephone, and distribution and sale of selected National Archives forms and publications. Guides to each regional archives' records and microfilm publications are available free of charge.

Most of the field office records that are part of the National Archives are in the various branches of the Federal Archives and Records Centers, which contain branch offices of departments of the federal government. Field office records include vital statistics, heirship, school, family register, census, and employment records.

Loretto Szucs, *The Archives: A Guide to the National Archives Field Branches* (Salt Lake City: Ancestry, 1988) gives detailed information regarding the holdings of the branches. Since many record groups have been relocated it is always best to call ahead to verify the whereabouts of the desired records.

A Selection of National Archives Publications Available Through the Family History Library System

The major record groups of the National Archives have been filmed and are circulated to Family History Centers. These include census schedules, both population and non-population; military records, including pension files, service records, muster rolls, orderly books, etc.; passenger manifests; passport applications; naturalization records; federal court records; land records (see chapter 3); customs records, and more.

Chapter 3
Federal Land Records
Bureau of Land Management, Eastern States
U.S. Geological Survey Library
The National Archives and Records Administration (NARA), "ARCHIVES I"
The National Archives at College Park (NAACP), "ARCHIVES II"

The National Archives and Bureau of Land Management have made numerous changes in the locations of their holdings. Most of the records of genealogical value held by the National Archives are scheduled to move to Archives I. These include all the land, bounty land, U.S. Court of Claims records, U.S. District Court records, and passport applications. While in transition, some record groups may be closed or divided between different locations. If in doubt as to where to find a record group, contact the Genealogy Staff at 202-501-5410.

The buildings that have been closed, or are closing, and the agencies that have relocated, are:

→ Cartographic Branch of the National Archives in Alexandria, VA, **now closed**.
→ National Archives Regional Records Center, Suitland, MD, **closing by December 1996**.
→ Bureau of Land Management, Eastern States, **relocated from Alexandria to Springfield, VA**.

For information on hours and access to the NARA facilities, please consult chapter 2. There is a shuttle that runs hourly between Archives I and Archives II.

AGENCIES OF THE DEPARTMENT OF THE INTERIOR

Bureau of Land Management, Eastern States

The Bureau of Land Management was formed in 1946 and became custodian of the records of the Government Land Office (GLO), which was itself established in 1812. Its holdings include about 7.5 million ownership titles, which cover 1.5 billion acres of land.

The BLM-ES is responsible for all the public land states adjoining or east of the Mississippi River. There are thirteen eastern public land states: Alabama, Arkansas, Florida, Illinois, Indiana, Iowa, Louisiana, Michigan, Minnesota, Mississippi, Missouri, Ohio, and Wisconsin. Patents, 10,000 tract books, card indexes, and survey field notes and plats are available to the researcher at BLM-ES. The total number of conveyance documents covers around five million homesteads, including cash sales, warrants, private land claims, swamp lists, state selections, and railroad lists.

☞ Location
Bureau of Land Management, Eastern States Office
7450 Boston Boulevard
Springfield, VA 22153-3197

☎ Phone
703-440-1600

🕐 Hours
7:30 AM–4:00 PM Mon-Fri

❖ New CD-ROM Products
The GLO Automated Records Project has begun digitizing the database of patents issued prior to 1908. Title records for the states of Arkansas, Louisiana, Florida, Michigan, Minnesota, Mississippi, Ohio, and Wisconsin have been completed. It is projected that the other eastern states should be ready by the end of

1996. These records can be accessed on site, or by researchers with modems, by registering with the Automated Records System. Retrieval /query sessions cost $2.00 a minute.

The major advantage of this new program is that it allows some records to be searched by the name of the patentee rather than just the legal description.

The GLO records for Arkansas, Florida, Louisiana, Michigan, and Wisconsin on CD-ROM are available and ready for purchase for $15.00 each. They can be purchased through the Government Printing Office. See the section in chapter 7 on the Government Printing Office for ordering information.

✎ Mail Requests
If you specify the legal description of the land, BLM-ES can locate the patent and supply you with a copy. BLM-ES can also supply you with copies of the field notes and plats. Copies are $4.25 per page. If your request for copies requires more than fifteen minutes search time, a charge of $4.80 per quarter hour will be made.

U.S. Geological Survey Library

Holdings include: 400,000 sheet maps; geologic and topographical maps from the 1850s to the present; 600,000 monographic and serial titles. There is a USGS Library Catalog available on CD-ROM, available on site and at many public libraries. The stacks in the library are open.

☞ Location
Geological Survey Library
12201 Sunrise Valley Drive
Reston, VA 22092-0523

☎ Phone
703-648-4302
703-648-5555 (Map Reference Librarian)

⏱ Hours
7:30 AM–4:15 PM Mon-Fri

→ Public Access
Open to the public by appointment.

✍ Publications
U.S. Geological Survey Library System, available free of charge.

Publications of the Geological Survey, 1879–1961.
Geographical Names Information System, Digital Gazetteer. The CD-ROM and user's manual are available for $59.00 by calling 1-800-USA-MAPS. This contains an index to place names, past and present.

✎ Mail Requests
To find the location of an obscure town or place name, current or historical, the U.S. Board on Geographic Names, at the Library, will provide free searches. Write to the Executive Secretary for Domestic Names at the above address.

PUBLIC LAND STATES

Land owned by the federal government is called "public domain." There are thirty public land states which were formed from the public domain.

Eastern States
Open (states with public land still available for purchase): Alabama, Arkansas, Florida, Louisiana, Michigan, Minnesota, Mississippi, and Wisconsin

Closed (states that no longer offer public land for sale): Illinois, Indiana, Iowa, Missouri, and Ohio

Western States
Alaska, Arizona, California, Colorado, Idaho, Kansas, Montana, Nebraska, Nevada, New Mexico, North Dakota, Oklahoma, Oregon, South Dakota, Utah, Washington, and Wyoming.

Federal land records pertain only to public domain lands. This automatically excludes the original thirteen colonies, which were not part of the acquisition of the westward expansion, plus Hawaii, Kentucky, Maine, Tennessee, Texas, West Virginia, and the District of Columbia. Inquiries concerning land records for these states should be directed to the individual state archives or land record offices. The National Archives and Library of Congress also have some early land records available on microfilm.

Location of Federal Land Records and Maps

Facility	Case Files	Patents	Tract Books	Notes/Plats	Maps
Archives I	Bounty Land Warrant Applications, Surrendered Bounty Land Warrants, Credit, Cash, Homestead, Donation, Timber, and Preemption, Private Land Claims		Western States		
Archives II				Eastern Closed States and Kansas	Enumeration District, Civil Division Outline, General Land Office, Pre-Federal, Corps of Engineers, County Outline, BIA
Bureau of Land Management, Eastern States		Eastern States and Bounty Land Warrants	Eastern States	Eastern Open States and Duplicate Western States	
Geological Survey Library					Topographic, Quadrangle
Library of Congress see chapter 4					U.S. Ward, Land Ownership

The Public Land Survey System of the United States

On 20 May 1785, the Continental Congress established the Public Land Survey System, based on a rectangular grid. The Treasury Board was then empowered to sell this public land to raise revenue.

Rectangular Land Survey System

Except for parts of Ohio, public land descrip-tions follow a uniform pattern. The country is marked off in standard east-west base lines and north-south meridians. Ranges are marked off east and west of meridians. Townships are marked off north and south of base lines.

The blackened township is T3N R2E—township three north of range two east.

A township is 6 miles square and is identified by township and range numbers, such as township 3 north, range 2 east. Each township is divided into 36 sections, which are numbered as follows:

6	5	4	3	2	1
7	8	9	10	11	12
18	17	16	15	14	13
19	20	21	22	23	24
30	29	28	27	26	25
31	32	33	34	35	36

A section contains 640 acres and can be divided into half sections [north half (N2), south half (S2), east half (E2), west half (W2)] and quarter sections [northwest quarter (NW4), northeast quarter (NE4), southeast quarter (SE4), southwest quarter (SW4)]. A quarter

section can be further divided into half-quarter sections, quarter-quarter sections, and fractional 5-acre lots.

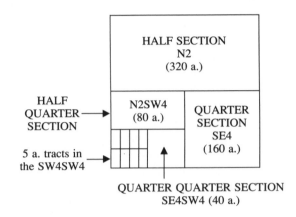

The "NE4SW4 Sec 24 T1N R10E 6PM" precisely identifies a certain 80 acres of land in West Branch Precinct, Pawnee Co., NE and is read "the northeast quarter of the southwest quarter of section 24 in township 1 north of range 10 east of the 6th principal meridian."

Tract Books

First developed around 1800 and maintained in local land offices, the tract books contain a record of all transactions involving public land. They are arranged by township and range and contain:

✓   Land description
✓   Number of acres
✓   Date of sale
✓   Purchase price
✓   Name of purchaser
✓   Type of sale
✓   Land office
✓   Entry number
✓   Final certificate number
✓   Notes on relinquishments and conversions

10,000 tract books for the eastern public land states, all of which adjoin the Mississippi River to the east, are located at BLM-ES.

Card indexes were made from the tract book entries and are available for the following ten states: Alabama, Arkansas, Illinois, Indiana, Iowa, Michigan, Minnesota, Mississippi, Ohio, and Wisconsin. These indexes are arranged by township and range within each state. The card indexes are easier to work with than the large, heavy tract books.

Once you have the information from either the cards or the tract books, you can get a copy of the patent or see the case file.

Tract books for the western states are located at Archives I. States included are Alaska, Arizona, California, Colorado, Idaho, Kansas, Montana, Nebraska, Nevada, Oklahoma, Oregon, South Dakota, Utah, Washington, and Wyoming. Because the tract books are arranged by township, range, and section, you need to know the specific location of the land.

Patents

A land patent is a document which conveys to the purchaser legal title to public lands. A patent contains:

✓   Name of purchaser
✓   Legal description of the land
✓   Law under which land was sold and
      patented
✓   Date of title
✓   President of U.S. at that time

Patents for the thirteen eastern states are on file at BLM-ES. Patents available include those issued for bounty land warrants. Patents for the public lands in the western states are maintained by BLM's eleven western offices. Contact the appropriate western office to obtain a copy of a patent.

Survey Field Notes and Plats

The first land records to develop from the Ordinance of 1785 were survey field notes. Survey field notes were prepared by the surveyor. They describe the survey performed and may include the names of settlers living in the survey area. They may also include descriptions of land formations, climate, soil, and plant and animal life.

Survey plats are drawings of the boundaries created by each survey and were prepared from the information in the field notes and sketches.

There are two types of township survey plats available: headquarters office plats and local office plats. The headquarters office plats show section numbers and boundaries. The local office plats are more detailed and are generally of greater use to the genealogist. The plats usually show land entry symbols and numbers and may possibly include the names of patentees.

Survey field notes and plats for the following eastern states are available at BLM-ES: Alabama, Arkansas, Florida, Louisiana, Michigan, Minnesota, Mississippi, and Wisconsin. These eight states are referred to as "open states," as they all contain public land that is currently for sale.

Notes and plats for the five eastern closed states that do not contain any more public land for sale, and Kansas, are at Archives II. Archives II has local office plats for the states of Illinois, Indiana, Iowa, Kansas, Missouri, and Ohio. It also has duplicate plats for parts of Alabama, Wisconsin, and Mississippi.

The original plats are at BLM-ES. In addition, there are local office plats for private land claims in several of the western states. See *List of Cartographic Records of the Government Land Office* (SL 19), available on site.

Notes and plats for the western states, except for Kansas, are filed with the eleven western offices, and BLM-ES has duplicate copies. The original copies are filed with the individual western state offices.

Copies can be made of these records. The field notes cost $4.00 for the first page and $1.00 per page thereafter from the same volume. The plats cost $4.00 each.

Case Files

Case files are the records of individual land sales and transactions. The case files for all states, 1800 to 1962, include the following types of records:

★   Cash entries
★   Credit entries
★   Homestead entries

★   Timber claims
★   Preemption claims
★   Private land claims
★   Donation land claims
★   Bounty land application files
★   Surrendered bounty land warrant files

Most land entry files prior to 1862, both cash and credit entries, contain little information other than the name of the entryman and his place of residence at the time of purchase. Bounty land warrant application files and those entry files after 1862—homestead, donation, timber, and preemption entries—are often rich in genealogical information.

Bounty land, credit, cash, homestead, donation, timber, and preemption files are located at Archives I.

Information needed to have file pulled:

✓   For cash, credit, and homestead
     entries and timber and preemption
     claims:
     Name of state
     Land office
     Type of entry
     Entry number
✓   For a surrendered bounty land
     warrant:
     File number
     Number of acres
     Act under which land was granted
✓   For private or donation land claims:
     Name of state
     File number

To View Case Files
Give the final certificate number, the type of entry, the name of the land office and the state to the staff member helping you. The staff member will then pull the file.

Credit Entry Files
Nearly all the land sold by the federal government between 1800 and mid-1820 was sold on credit at no less than $2.00 per acre. The sale of land on credit was discontinued after 30 June 1820. However, many who had previously purchased land and who were behind in their payments were able to obtain title to their land

through various relief acts. Once the purchase of the land was complete, the purchaser received a credit entry final certificate. These certificates fall into two categories, depending upon when the purchase was completed:

★   *Credit Prior.* Certificate issued for a
     purchase completed prior to 1 July
     1820
★   *Credit Under.* Certificate issued for a
     purchase completed after 1 July 1820
     under relief legislation

A final certificate usually shows:

✓   Name of entryman
✓   Place of residence of entryman as
     given at the time of purchase
✓   Date of purchase
✓   Number of acres in tract
✓   Legal description of tract
✓   Summary of payments made
✓   Page and volume number of the
     record copy in the Bureau of Land
     Management

Cash Entry Files
Nearly all of the land sold by the federal government to individual settlers after 30 June 1820 was sold for cash at no less than $1.25 per acre. A complete cash entry file includes:

✓   Application for tract of land
✓   Receipt for monies paid
✓   Final certificate which authorized the
     claimant to obtain a patent. This
     contains the same information as the
     credit entry final certificate.

If the tract of land was claimed on the basis of a preemption claim, the file may also include a *preemption proof.* If the tract of land was originally entered as a homestead, and the homestead entry had been commuted to a cash entry, the file includes the *homestead entry file.*

Homestead Entry Files
Under the terms of the Homestead Act of 1862, a citizen, or a person who had filed his intention to become a citizen, twenty-one years of age or older, was eligible to claim 160 acres of unoccupied land on the public domain, provid-

HOMESTEADERS IN MICHIGAN, ca 1885

ing he fulfilled certain requirements. The provisions of the act required that the homesteader build a home on the land, cultivate the land, and reside there for five years. The following documents may be found in a file:

✓ Homestead application, including:
   name of entryman
   place of residence at time of application
   legal description of the land
   number of acres
   certification of publication of intention to make claim
✓ Homestead proof, including:
   testimony of two witnesses and entryman
   legal description of the land
   name, age, PO address of entryman
   description of house and first date of residence
   number and relationship of family members
   nature of crops
   number of acres under cultivation
✓ Final certificate, which includes:
   name, PO address of entryman
   legal description of land
   date patent issued
   BLM volume and page reference numbers
✓ Copy of naturalization proceedings, which may include:
   name of immigrant
   date and port of arrival
   place of birth
✓ Copy of Union veteran's discharge

Preemption and Timber Entry Files

A man could, without permission, settle on public land, build a house, and make other improvements. When the adjoining land was put up for public sale, he could purchase as much as 160 acres of land at $1.25 per acre. This was called a preemption claim. A man could apply for up to 160 additional acres of land from the government in exchange for planting ten acres of timber-producing trees. This was called a timber claim.

Locating Credit, Cash, Homestead, Preemption, and Timber Files

State Known: For patents awarded after 30 June 1908 there is a name index at Archives I. There is also a name index for patents 1800 to 30 June 1908 for land in the following states: Alabama, Alaska, Arizona, Florida, Louisiana, Nevada, and Utah.

For other patents before 30 June 1908 you need the land office, type of entry, and final certificate number. To find this information, obtain the legal land description from the county recorder's office. Without the legal description you can find the information, but the search will take longer. You need to know the township or the county in which the land was located. This information can be found in the census records.

Legal Land Description Known: With the legal description, go directly to the tract books or card files and obtain the information necessary to identify the file.

EXAMPLE: NW4 Section 24, Township 1 North, Range 10 East, Pawnee County, Nebraska

Because Nebraska is a western state, this search will be done at Archives I. Request the tract book containing the above township and range. Turn to the beginning of Township 1 North, Range 10 East, and look for Section 24. Sections are listed numerically in order. Within Section 24, search for either the land description or the name. Copy the information from the entry. To have the case file pulled you need the land office, the type of entry, and the final certificate number.

Township Only Known: If you know the township in which the land is located but do not have the legal description, you will have to look through all the entries for the entire township.

EXAMPLE: Boone Township, Crawford County, Indiana

Because Indiana is an eastern state, this search will be done at BLM-ES. Obtain the township and range numbers from the large atlas in the search room—Township 4 South, Range 1 East.

The cards will be separated by dividers marked with the township and range numbers. Because you do not know what section the land is in, you must look through all the cards in the 4S/1E division to find the one you want. To have the case file pulled, you need the land office, type of entry, and final certificate number. For a state with no card file, the procedure is the same, except that you will look at a tract book instead of a card file.

County Only Known: If you know only the county in which the land is located, your search is widened considerably. You will have to look through all the entries for the entire county.

EXAMPLE: Pawnee County, Nebraska

Because Nebraska is a western state, this search will be done at Archives I. Obtain the township and range numbers for the entire county from the large atlas in the search room.

Request the tract book or books containing all of these townships. Because you do not know which township the land is in, you must search all townships and all sections within each township to find the purchaser's name. To have the case file pulled, you need the land office, type of entry, and final certificate number.

For a state with a card file, the procedure is the same, except that you will look at cards instead of tract books.

Donation Files

During certain times and under certain conditions of settlement, certain lands were given away to settlers. Donation lands were in Florida, Oregon, and Washington.

Florida Donation Entry Files

These files are indexed and are located at Archives I. A complete file includes:

✓ Permit to settle, containing:
   name of applicant
   marital status
   month/year became resident of Florida
   legal description of land
✓ Application for patent, containing:
   name of applicant
   legal description of land
   name of settler
   period of his settlement
✓ Report by land agent
✓ Final certificate authorizing claimant to obtain a patent, containing:
   name of applicant
   legal description of land
   date of patent
   volume/page numbers of the BLM copy

Oregon and Washington Donation Files (M815)

These files are indexed. A complete file has:

✓ Notification on the settlement of public land, including:
   legal description of land
   name of entryman
   place of residence at time of notification
   citizenship
   date and place of birth
   given name of wife
   date and place of marriage
✓ Donation certificate, including:
   name of entryman
   place of residence
   legal description of land
   date of patent
   volume and page number of record copy in BLM

The original records and microfilmed copies are available at Archives I. The abstracts are also available and serve as indexes to the files:

★ *Abstracts of Oregon Donation Land Claims 1852–1903* (M145)

★   *Abstracts of Washington Donation Land Claims 1855–1902* (M203)
★   *Oregon and Washington Donation Land Claim Files* (M815)

Private Land Claim Records

These claims were made by persons, or their descendants, who were granted land by foreign governments or who had claims to land that eventually came into the U.S. public domain. There are records of private land claims and their case files at Archives I for parts of the following states:

Florida Cession: Florida
Louisiana Purchase: Arkansas, Iowa, Louisiana, and Missouri
Mexican Cession: Arizona, California, Colorado, and New Mexico
Mississippi Territory: Alabama and Mississippi
Northwest Territory: Illinois, Indiana, Michigan, and Wisconsin

The private land claims case files have indexes for most areas. Files vary greatly in content. The following items may be found in a case file:

✓   Correspondence
✓   Reports
✓   Maps and plats
✓   Petitions
✓   Affidavits
✓   Court decision transcriptions
✓   Deeds and/or title abstracts
✓   Wills
✓   Marriage certificates

An eight-volume series, *American State Papers, Public Lands,* contains transcribed records relating to individual claims presented before federal agencies, 1790–1837. Each volume is indexed by name of claimant. There is also a consolidated index entitled *Grassroots of America,* by Philip McMullin (Salt Lake City: Gendex, 1972). These volumes and indexes are available in Room 203 in Archives I.

MAPS

The National Archives has custody of nearly two million maps. Several series are of particular use to the genealogist and can be used in Archives II.

→ Photoduplication

Tabs are available for marking pages to be copied. Copies are $.25 each if the staff does the copying, $.10 each on the self-service copying machines. The staff will not make copies while you wait. You must fill out an order blank, pay in advance, and leave the tabbed documents to be copied later if you want the staff to do the copying. Your copies will be mailed within four to six weeks after your visit.

✎ Mail requests

Describe in detail the maps you want. You will be sent a "Quotation for Reproduction Services" form by return mail listing the items you want and the price for each. To order, simply check the items you want, enclose a check for the proper amount (payable to National Archives Trust Fund), and send everything to the address on the form. There is a minimum order fee of $6.00.

Oversized electrostatic copies of maps can be made. The average cost of reproducing a map is $5.00. Prices will vary according to the size of the maps to be copied. Photographic reproductions are also available but are more expensive. You can pay with cash, check, money order, or travelers check.

❦ Resources Available

The following is a brief outline of the large collection of maps at Archives II:

Census Enumeration District (ED) Maps 1880–1970

ED maps show the boundaries and numbers of each enumeration district. Maps for western states start at 1900. If the census is unindexed or if you cannot find a person in the index, knowing the enumeration district can facilitate finding the person in the census records.

Obtain the person's address from a city directory and find the address on the proper ED map.

Once you determine the correct ED for the address you can go directly to the census and search for the individual.

Preliminary Inventory of the Cartographic Records of the Bureau of the Census (PI 103) lists by year which ED maps are available for which locations.

Census Enumeration District (ED) Descriptions 1850–1950
The ED descriptive rolls are written descriptions identifying the districts used in taking the various censuses. These rolls are also available on microfilm in Room 400 of Archives I.

Civil Division Outline Maps 1920–1970 (Post Office)
There are 500 annotated maps of the U.S. and individual states. These maps show county or municipality and minor civil division boundaries, and names and locations of unincorporated places.

Maps of States and Territories (General Land Office)
This is a listing of manuscript and published maps of states and territories, some of which (primarily Ohio, Indiana, and Illinois) show individual land districts.

Most of these maps were compiled from official sources during the nineteenth century. They usually show the locations of land offices and the boundaries of land districts, private land claims, counties, and federal land reserves. Maps of individual land districts sometimes show townships with names of landowners in numbered sections.

This is good for general reference, but not specific information. The finding aid for these maps is *List of Selected Maps of States and Territories* (SL 29), which is available on site.

Pre-Federal Maps
Copies and several originals of seventeenth-and eighteenth-century maps are on file at Archives II. *Pre-Federal Maps in the National Archives: An Annotated List* (SL 26) provides a catalog to this collection, and is available on site.

U.S. Army Corps of Engineers Maps
These maps often show roads, canals, and waterways that were used as migration routes. They contain names of mountains, churches, mills, etc. They sometimes show land ownership or names of residents. Also included are maps of Civil War battlefields with names of owners or residents of the properties.

County Outline Maps 1840–1900
These maps were published by the Department of Agriculture. Check these maps for county boundaries and names as they existed for a specific census year.

Bureau of Indian Affairs Maps
Maps pertaining to Indian treaties, removal policy, land use, reservations, and settlements are on file with the BLM. Consult *List of Cartographic Records in the Bureau of Indian Affairs* (SL 13), available on site.

A Selection of Resources Available Through the Family History Library System

When a researcher looks for a map of a particular town or county, the logical place to start is in the catalog under the town or city. There are some resources in the Family History Library Catalog that are not cataloged under the state locality, but are only found in general U.S. land records. This makes searching difficult, but with some detective work, they can be "unearthed."

Topographical Maps of the United States, U. S. Geological Survey

291 microfilm reels: 1433631–1433921
These are the quadrangle maps of all U.S. states and territories.

Bureau of Land Management Card Files, Eastern States Office

160 microfilm reels: 1501522–1501681

The card files are finding-aids to locate patent documents in the BLM. By using these files, researchers are able to get the land office name and certificate number and can eliminate several steps in locating federal land records. Each card contains the following information:

✓ Certificate number
✓ District land office
✓ Kind of entry (cash, credit, warrant, etc.)
✓ Name of patentee, county of origin
✓ Land description
✓ Number of acres
✓ Date of patent
✓ Volume and page where document can be located

States included: Alabama, Arkansas, Illinois, Indiana, Iowa, Minnesota, Missouri, Ohio, and Wisconsin

Field Notes from Selected General Land Office Township Surveys

281 microfilm reels: 1065501–1065781

This filming is the reproduction of the volumes of field notes from the original surveys of six states. The notes contain detailed descriptions on running the township and section lines, topography, natural vegetation, and potential uses of the land. Index maps for each state locate the numbered volumes for each township.

States included: Illinois, Indiana, Iowa, Kansas, Missouri, and Ohio

Township Plats of Selected States, Bureau of Land Management

67 microfilm reels: 1578331–1578397

The townships were surveyed by the General Land Office (now the Bureau of Land Management) between 1795 and 1887. The plats contain information about the original sale or disposition of each parcel of land to the first landholder, or entryman.

States included: Alabama, Illinois, Indiana, Iowa, Kansas, Mississippi, Missouri, Oklahoma, Wisconsin, Ohio, Oregon, and Washington.

Land Ownership Maps, Library of Congress, Geography and Map Division

2,010 microfiche: 6079238–6081631

County land ownership maps are invaluable in tracing family backgrounds. This set contains the LOC collection of pre-twentieth century (1840–1890) land ownership maps, including 1,449 county maps.

States included: north central states, northeastern states, Virginia, California, and Texas.

Ward Maps of the U.S., Library of Congress, Geography and Map Division

3,020 microfiche
1 microfilm reel: 1377700

All the maps on the microfiche are contained on one reel of film. The earliest maps are 1794 (Albany, NY) and the latest are 1899 (Cleveland, OH). The cities included are:

Albany, NY	Kansas City, MO
Allegheny, PA	Louisville, KY
Atlanta, GA	Memphis, TN
Baltimore, MD	Milwaukee, WI
Boston, MA	Minneapolis, MN
Brooklyn, NY	New Haven, CT
Buffalo, NY	New Orleans, LA
Charleston, SC	New York, NY
Chicago, IL	Newark, NJ
Cincinnati, OH	Philadelphia, PA
Cleveland, OH	Providence, RI
Columbus, OH	Richmond, VA
Denver, CO	Rochester, NY
Detroit, MI	St. Louis, MO
Hartford, CT	St. Paul , MN
Indianapolis, IN	San Francisco, CA
Jersey City, NJ	Washington, DC

Chapter 4
The Library of Congress (LC)

Introduction

☞ Location

Across the street from the U.S. Capitol. Contained in three buildings, connected by a tunnel system.

Thomas Jefferson Building: 1st Street, SE, between East Capitol Street and Independence Avenue.

James Madison Memorial Building: Independence Avenue between 1st and 2nd Streets, SE.

John Adams Building: 2nd Street, SE between East Capitol Street and Independence Avenue.

The tunnel is on the cellar level in the Jefferson and Adams Buildings and on the ground level in the Madison Building.

☎ Phone

General number: 202-707-5000; 202-707-6200 TTD
General fax number: 202-707-5844
Reference telephone numbers: 202-707-5522; 202-707-4210 TTD; Fax: 202-507-1389
Cataloging Distribution Service: 800-255-3666 or 202-707-6100; Fax 202-707-1334

Recorded information numbers:
202-707-6400 (reading room hours)
202-707-6500 (researchers)
202-707-8000 (visitors)
202-707-4700 (directions)

🕐 Hours

Information Desk: 8:30 AM–9:30 PM Mon-Fri; 8:30 AM–6:00 PM Sat
Local History and Genealogy Reading Room, Main Reading Room, Microform Reading Room, Newspaper and Current Periodical Reading Room: 8:30 AM–9:30 PM Mon, Wed, Thu; 8:30 AM–5:00 PM Tue, Fri, Sat

Geography and Map Reading Room: 8:30 AM–9:30 PM Mon-Fri
Machine Readable Collection Reading Room: 12:00 PM–4:00 PM Mon-Fri
Photoduplication Service: 9:00 AM–4:45 PM Mon-Fri

Ⓢ Public Transportation and Parking
Metro: The Capitol South Metro Station, serviced by both the Blue and Orange Lines, is at 1st and C Streets, SE. Walk north along 1st Street towards Independence Avenue and the Capitol. The Madison Building is on the right. Walk across Independence Avenue to get to the Jefferson Building.

Bus Service: Several bus routes serve Capitol Hill.

Parking: Limited parking is available at two-hour meters between 9:30 AM and 6:00 PM. Meters take quarters only. Before leaving the car, make sure it is not in a restricted area or a tow-away zone. Also, make a note of where it is. DC police have spent many hours helping visitors find their "misplaced" cars. Areas marked "Reserved Government Parking" may be used Saturdays and Sundays and after 5:00 PM weekdays.

The Library encourages researchers to use public transportation.

→ Public Access
The Library of Congress is open to the public and to researchers over the age of eighteen. Photo ID is required for researchers. An LC User card can be obtained at the Information Desk of the Main Reading Room. The Library of Congress is a closed stack library. No library materials may be removed from any of the Library's reading rooms.

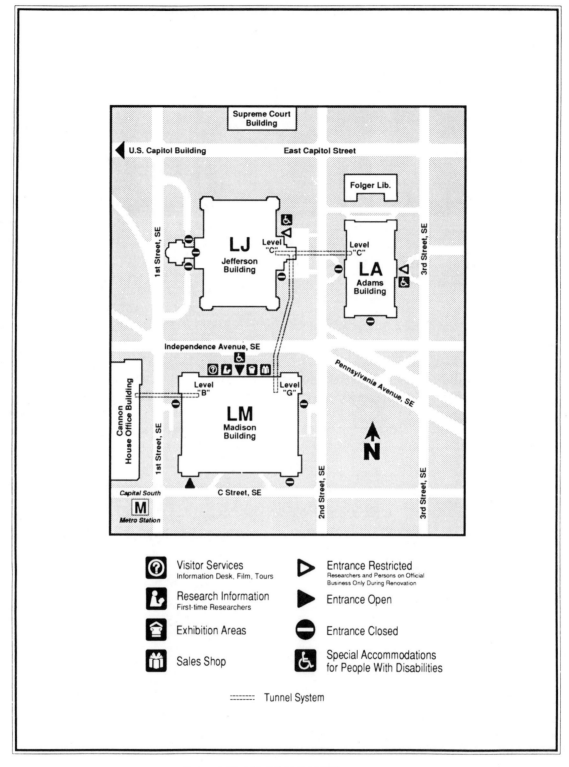

LIBRARY OF CONGRESS

Personal property is inspected by the Library police upon entrance and departure. Silent notebook computers may be used in designated areas of reading rooms. A limited number of lockers are available in the Jefferson Building and some of the specialized reading rooms. Access and equipment for the disabled are available.

→ Photoduplication
Photoduplication is available through self-service coin operated and debit card copiers. Cost is $.10 by copy card and $.15 by coin for standard size copies. All photocopiers and most microfilm reader/printers take both coins and copy cards. Use only LC copy cards in LC card readers.

To obtain cards or to add value to cards, see instructions on the automatic copy card dispenser. The card costs $1.00 and already includes $1.80 worth of credit. The initial purchase must be $1.00. Higher denominations are accepted on initial purchase. Visa, MasterCard, Discover, and American Express are accepted after initial purchase.

❖ Online Database Services
LOCIS (Library of Congress Online Information System)
locis.loc.gov or 140.147.254.3
Instructions to connect to LOCIS: 202-707-3636
LC MARVEL (Library of Congress Campus-Wide Information System)
marvel.loc.gov. or 140.147.2.69, login marvel
Gopher server: **marvel.loc.gov, port 70**

✎ Requests by Mail
Maps
Library of Congress
Geography and Map Division
Washington, DC 20540

> **Note:** When writing for a photocopy of a map, be as specific as possible with the description. Enclose a photocopy of the reference cited and a daytime phone number in case there are questions regarding the request.
>
> It is not possible for the Geography and Map Division to undertake extensive research projects; however, they will respond to requests that cannot be answered by a local library.

Photoduplication Service
Library of Congress
Photoduplication Service
Washington, DC 20540-5230

Publications
Library of Congress
Catalog Distribution Service
Customer Services Division
Washington, DC 20540-5017

✍ Publications
Genealogical Research at the Library of Congress (Washington, DC: U.S. Government Printing Office, October 1992).

Reference Services and Facilities of the Local History and Genealogy Reading Room (Washington, DC: Library of Congress Humanities and Social Sciences Division, August 1994).

Information for Researchers: Using the Library of Congress (Washington, DC: Library of Congress Humanities and Social Sciences Division, 1995).

Mann, Thomas. *Doing Research at the Library of Congress: A Guide to Subject Searching in a Closed Stacks Library* (Washington, DC: Library of Congress Humanities and Social Sciences Division, 1994).

Walsh. Barbara B. *Telephone and City Directories in the Library of Congress: A Finding Guide* (Washington, DC: Library of Congress Humanities and Social Sciences Division, Local History and Genealogy Team. No. 18. November 1994).

The Humanities and Social Sciences Division distributes free upon request short bibliographies related to genealogical research.

→ Food and Beverages
Madison Building
Cafeteria—6th floor
9:00 AM–10:30 AM breakfast Mon-Fri
12:30 PM–3:00 PM lunch Mon-Fri
Coffee Shop—ground floor
9:00 AM–4:00 PM Mon-Fri
8:30 AM–2:00 PM Sat
Food or beverages may only be consumed in

the cafeteria and coffee shop. Vending machines are available in all buildings.

General Information

The Library of Congress was established in 1800 as a Congressional resource. Originally located in the U.S. Capitol, it was destroyed when the British burned the building in 1814. To rebuild the collection, Thomas Jefferson offered his 6,500 volume library at cost. Currently, the book collections are the most comprehensive in the areas of U.S. and foreign public documents, law, history, political science, sociology, language, literature, technology and science, and bibliography.

The growth of the Library led to the construction of a separate facility, the Thomas Jefferson Building, constructed in 1897. The Adams Building was completed in 1939, and the Madison Building in 1980. The Jefferson Building is presently being restored; the estimated date of completion is 1997. At that time, some of the reading rooms will be relocated to more spacious quarters.

In addition to the Jefferson restoration, future plans include continuing expansion of the use of electronic media. Since 1993, the Library has provided free access on the Internet to twenty-eight million bibliographic records. As part of the National Digital Library effort, five million images from the American History Collection are currently being digitized. Some other ongoing projects are the expanded use of optical disks to store, index, retrieve, and duplicate records; mass deacidification of disintegrating photographs and films; and the acquisition of additional storage space for three million more volumes (see Stephen E. Ostrow and Robert Zich, *Research Collections in the Information Age: The Library of Congress Looks to the Future*. Washington, DC: Library of Congress, 1990). Although the primary function of the Library of Congress is to serve the Congress of the United States, the Library also welcomes public use of its general reference facilities.

The Library contains many publications and records that are valuable for genealogical research, including the following:

- American and foreign genealogies
- City directories and telephone directories
- Maps and atlases
- Newspapers
- Manuscript collections
- Periodicals published by state historical societies
- Histories of localities in the U.S. and foreign countries
- Book/microfilm records on immigration/emigration
- Guides to records in state archival agencies and historical societies
- CD-ROM products, including directories, encyclopedias, and indexes

Facts and Figures

Items in collection: over 108 million

Number of volumes printed before 1500: 5,600

Total books: over 26 million

Number of languages in repository: 460

Map collection: over 4 million pieces

World's largest collections: Hispanic and Arabic

Largest collection outside of native country: Russian and Chinese

Reels of film: over 500,000

Number of accessions per day: 7,000, mostly through copyright deposits

Total shelf space of holdings: over 500 miles

The Thomas Jefferson Building "LJ"

The facilities in the LJ that are of interest to the genealogical researcher are the:

→ Local History and Genealogy Reading Room
→ Main Reading Room
→ European Reading Room
→ Hispanic Reading Room
→ Folklife Reading Room

→ Rare Book and Special Collections
   Reading Room
→ Microform Reading Room
→ Machine Readable Collections
   Reading Room

The best way to find out if a division has information that will be pertinent to any genealogical search is to visit the Local History and Genealogy Reading Room. The reference staff and library attendants can save hours of random searching for the beginning researcher. They will help determine where the records can be found and refer the patron to the appropriate reading room, if necessary.

Local History and Genealogy Reading Room (LJ-G20)

The Local History and Genealogy Reading Room (LH&G) is located on the ground floor in the LJ. Some of the resources available in the LH&G are:

★ Guidebooks and manuals on general and ethnic research
★ Vital records guides
★ Directories of organizations and societies
★ Periodical indexes
★ Published census materials
★ Published genealogies, town and county histories
★ FamilySearch® on CD-ROM

Most of the collections and catalogs in LH&G will help with research in the United States. For foreign genealogy/local history, check the Family Name Catalog (white labels) in the LH&G. If that is not successful, try the computer catalog. Computer terminals and operating instructions are located near the main desk. Check the shelves by the main desk area for informative, free pamphlets.

Procedure

The stack areas in the LH&G reading room are open to the public. These stacks contain books of a general nature. Each stack is marked with the books it contains. In addition, there are lists of the stack holdings attached to the fronts of several of the stacks.

The stack areas beyond the reading room are closed to the public. Check the card catalog for the books you want and fill out a call slip for each one. Be sure to include your desk number on the slip. Patrons are limited to fifteen requests per hour.

When ordering a book for use in the LH&G, use an LH&G call slip. If you use a Main Reading Room call slip, your book will be delivered there. LH&G call slips are brown; Main Reading Room slips are blue.

When the call slips are filled out, take them to the Book Service Desk in the reading room. The books will be delivered to your desk.

If the books are unavailable, the call slips will be returned. Check the lower right corner of a returned slip for the explanation. If the slip is marked "not on shelf," recheck your information for accuracy. Resubmit the call slip and ask for a check of the Central Charge File (CCF). This will determine whether the book is on loan, in a reference collection, or on microfilm.

If the response from CCF is "NC" (no charge), take the slip to the Special Search Section in Alcove 1 of the Main Reading Room. A search for the book will be initiated, and you will be notified of the results.

If you cannot wait after turning in your call slips, check "overnight" in the box provided. Print your last name on the line below the box. Your books will be delivered to the call room and held overnight under your name.

You may reserve five books for three days by inserting the yellow slips (available at the Book Service Desk) and then shelving the books on the *three day reserve* shelf. *Reference books may not be reserved.*

The longest delays in delivering books occur during peak academic periods and on afternoons and Saturdays. Books must also be requested no later than one hour prior to closing.

Card Catalogs

There are seven specialized card catalogs:

★ Family Name Index. *(White Labels)* Arranged alphabetically by surname and chronologically by date of publication within each surname. This catalog was published in two volumes as *Genealogies in the Library of Congress,* by Marion J. Kaminkow (Baltimore: Magna Carta Book Co., 1971). In 1977, 1989, and 1992 supplements were published. These volumes are available in most large libraries.

★ Analyzed Surname Index. *(Green Labels)* Selected works, consisting mainly of county histories analyzed for brief references to surnames and individuals through about 1910. This index is not comprehensive. Check the last drawer entitled "Local Histories Indexed" to find out which county histories have been included in the index.

★ U.S. Biographical Index. *(Pink Labels)* Arranged alphabetically by surname. This index is not comprehensive. However, at least one book has been indexed from each state. Check the first drawer entitled "Books Indexed" for a list of the books included. There are no recent entries.

★ Coats-of-arms Index. Arranged alphabetically by surname. This index covers primarily British and American families. Technically, a coat-of-arms is to be used only by the eldest son of the eldest son back to the original bearer.

★ Subject Catalog. A three-volume local history and genealogy reference collection catalog.

★ Local History Shelf List. Arranged by classification numbers from F1 to F1000. At the beginning of every state drawer is a section entitled "Biography and Genealogy, Collected." Within this section will be found entire state collections. Cataloging is by subject. A large chart, "Guide to Materials in United States Local History," is near the catalog.

★ Computer Catalog. It is necessary to use the computer catalog for books that have been added since 1980. Instructions are located at the terminals in the reading rooms.

City Directories, Non-Current

The Library has the largest collection of city directories in the world. Some of these are available in the original, while others are available on microfilm or microfiche. The microfilm and microfiche copies are in the Microform Reading Room. The original city directories are kept in the closed stack area on deck 43. Put in request slips for them.

EXAMPLE: You need the 1910 New York City census for a person, but the census is not indexed.

Consult the 1910 and 1911 New York City directories and find the person's address. With this information you can go to the National Archives, use the 1910 New York City Enumeration District Index, and find the person on the 1910 census.

EXAMPLE: A person lived and died in Baltimore, MD. You want to obtain a death certificate for him, but you have no idea when he died.

Start with a year the person was alive (census records will help). Follow him through the directories each year until he disappears. You may find him listed one year and only his widow listed the following year. You will then have an approximate date of death and can send for a death certificate.

There is no comprehensive list which details the entire city directory collection. However, there is a notebook in the LH&G room which contains several lists that will help you determine which cities have directories. In addition to the old city directories, there are also old telephone directories.

✎ Mail Requests
While the LH&G staff members do not conduct complicated or lengthy research, they will check catalogs and indexes for specific items and suggest further research avenues. If specific information from a particular work is needed, the staff will examine the index to identify the family, individual, or fact which is sought.

The staff will send a limited number of photocopies of relevant material to the requester free of charge. Otherwise, the request will be referred to the Photoduplication Service, which will in turn advise of the fee for copying the information requested.

Main Reading Room (LJ-100)

Stop here and check on the informative, free pamphlets at the User Information Desk just inside the main entrance. The Main Reading Room is located on the first floor of the LJ.

Procedure
The Reference Assistance Room is staffed by reference librarians who will answer questions and offer assistance in locating research materials.

General Catalogs
The main card catalog contains subject, author, and title cards for most books cataloged by the Library through 1980.

The principal access to the Library's general collection is through the MUMS and SCORPIO search systems. There are complete instructions at each computer terminal. The touch screens for the computer catalog are easy to use. The staff will help if there are any questions. In the Computer Catalog Center there are classes to sign up for training on the Library of Congress computer systems.

Current Telephone, Street Address, and City Directories
On deck 46, behind Alcove 4, are the current telephone directories (both white and yellow pages), reverse telephone directories (street address directories), and city directories. Since many directories contain listings for more than one community, be sure to check the card catalog, which is located at the beginning of the collection.

The directories are filed alphabetically by state. Within each state division are the telephone directories first, the city directories second, and the reverse telephone directories third. To use U.S. telephone directories, consult Phone Fiche's *Community Cross Reference Index.* An alternate way to look up current phone numbers is by using *Phone Disc USA,* a CD-ROM product located in the Machine Readable Collections Reading Room (LJ G22).

Foreign directories follow U.S. directories and are filed alphabetically. For directories in Canada, the United Kingdom, and Switzerland, consult the *City Directory Finding Guide* at the Reference Desk in the LH&G. This guide also has information on U.S. directories on film from 1861 to 1935.

Rare Book and Special Collections Reading Room (LJ-206)

Many published genealogies and local U.S. histories have been transferred to the Rare Book Room for safekeeping. These books are identified by the word "OFFICE" marked on the cards in the LH&G catalog. Do not fill out a call slip for the book. Go to the Rare Book Room to request the book. The Rare Book Room is located on the second floor of the LJ.

Procedure
Sign the Register of Investigators in the outer area. Fill out the Reader's Registration Form for Use of Rare Materials. Coats, briefcases, and oversized handbags are not allowed in the Rare Book Room. There are lockers outside in the hallway for storing belongings. Only pencils may be used in the room.

Complete a book request sheet, listing the books you wish to see. You will be allowed up to five

MAIN READING ROOM

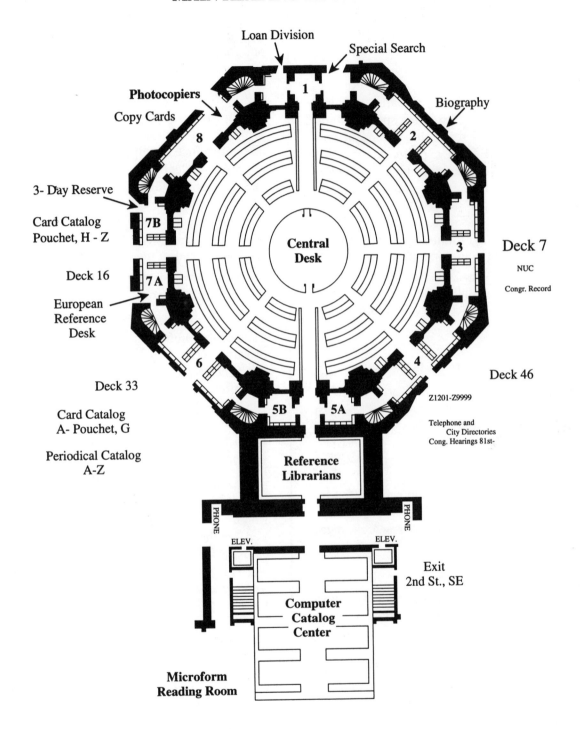

books at any one time. The book request sheet will be kept at the Charge Desk. More books will be given to you as you are ready for them.

Return books to the Charge Desk. The attendant will check off and initial each book entry on the book request sheet. Copies can be made by the Photoduplication Service only if the condition of the book will permit copying.

❧ Resources Available

In addition to the genealogies and county histories transferred here from the LH&G, the Rare Book Room also contains special collections of genealogical interest. The best known is the Charles Edward Banks Manuscript Collection, thirty-four volumes on colonial Massachusetts families. This collection has also been microfilmed and is available in the Microform Reading Room.

Microform Reading Room (LJ-107)

Many family and local U.S. histories have been filmed for preservation. These books are identified as microfilmed in the LH&G card catalog and can be viewed in the Microform Reading Room. The Microform Reading Room has a small incomplete card catalog titled "Genealogy." The Microform Reading Room is located on the first floor of the LJ.

Procedure

Fill out a call slip for the films you want. The films will be delivered in ten to twenty minutes to the table in the front of the room. Self-service copiers are available in the room.

Microfilm and microfiche copies of city directories are available in the Microform Reading Room. Select the film you need filed under the city name and use the available readers.

❧ Resources Available

In addition to the family genealogies and county histories that have been microfilmed for preservation, the collection includes a variety of transcripts, indexes, directories, scrapbooks, narratives, manuscripts, and other material of interest to the genealogist. On the open shelves you will find several guides and indexes, including the following:

★ *Guide to Microfilm Records of Early State Records.*
★ *Short Title Catalog of English Books,* 1475 to 1640 and 1641 to 1700. About 90 percent of these are available.
★ *British Manuscripts Project,* ninth through eighteenth centuries. Scan through entries 192–196 and 294. Check the table of contents for documents from the Public Record Office: 13 Colonies.
★ Typed index to National Society, Daughters of Founders and Patriots of America collection of genealogical material (film #5664).
★ Typed Index to *Genealogy of the Signers of the Declaration of Independence* (film #4498).
★ Typed Index to *Irish Genealogy* (films #1616 and #1617). These records cover the period 1588 to 1904 and consist of records gathered at the county level after the Dublin fire of 1922. Some are in such a confusing state that they are labeled "Chaos."
★ Challen Typescripts: London area transcripts of parish registers.
★ Hollingsworth Genealogical Card File: families from the southern U.S. states, with an emphasis on Georgia.
★ Biographical scrapbooks from the Metropolitan Central Library, Toronto, Ontario.
★ Slave Narratives from the Federal Writers Project. These are the original manuscripts on twelve rolls of microfilm.

James Madison Memorial Building "LM"

The facilities in the LM that are of interest to the genealogical researcher are the:

→ Manuscript Reading Room
→ Newspaper and Current Periodical Reading Room
→ Prints and Photographs Reading Room
→ Performing Arts Reading Room

→   Law Library Reading Room
→   Visitor's Orientation Theater and
      Tours (LM 139)

The Performing Arts Reading Room would only be of genealogical value if the subject or family being researched had a professional or career history that could be traced. The Prints and Photographs Reading Room can provide information on period photos that are available to be copied for a family history or other publication. Unless the ancestor in question was famous (or infamous), the likelihood of finding him or her in this collection is extremely remote.

If time allows, the twenty-one minute presentation about the Library is worth seeing. There are first come, first served tours of the Library that begin every half hour. Contact the Visitor Service Office for tour information.

Manuscript Reading Room (LM-101)

There are over thirty-five million manuscripts, documents, and personal papers available for use by researchers in the Manuscript Reading Room. Call several weeks in advance to make sure the manuscripts will be available. The Manuscript Reading Room is located on the first floor of the LM.

Procedure
Bring photo-identification to enable you to complete the Manuscript Division's registration form. Pencils, brief notes, and wallets can be taken into the reading room. Also personal computers, tape recorders, and cameras that do not require heat, rollers, light, or a wet process may be used by readers *under supervision*. Paper, upon approval, is provided for your use in the reading room. Free lockers are available for personal items not necessary for research.

Sign in at the security desk. Go to the main desk and tell the librarian what records you want to see. You will be directed to the proper finding aid and given a request form to fill out. Return all materials to the main desk when you have finished. If you need additional research time, notify a staff member. The materials can be held for three days. Staff historians specializing in early American history are available for consultation.

☙ Resources Available
Among the millions of manuscripts available are the following of special interest to genealogists:

★   Alaskan Russian church records, 1772–1936
★   Lyman C. Draper Collection, 1785–1815
★   Hamburg passenger lists, 1850–1873
★   George Washington Papers (Virginia militia records)
★   Foreign copying program (reproduction of records from foreign archives including British, French, Spanish, etc.)
★   WPA records (life histories, Mormon diaries, and slave narratives)
★   Personal and family papers, diaries, and journals

There is no consolidated index for the manuscript collection; however, there are unpublished catalogs and several finding aids available for consultation. They include:

★   *The National Union Catalog of Manuscript Collections*
★   *Manuscripts on Microfilm: A Checklist of the Holdings in the Manuscript Division*
★   *Manuscript Sources in the Library of Congress for Research on the American Revolution*

Newspaper and Current Periodical Reading Room (LM-133)

This room houses current and past issues of newspapers (both in hard copy and on microfilm) and unbound issues of current periodicals. The Newspaper Room is located on the first floor of the LM.

Procedure
Bring photo-identification. There is no sign-in procedure for this room. Fill out a call slip for each record you need, being sure to indicate your desk number.

Select any roll of film you want and take it to a vacant reader. When you are finished with the film, return it to the top of the cabinet where it belongs. Do not refile films.

Newspapers in hard copy are in storage, and a one-day advance request is necessary to have them delivered to the reading room. You may want to call the day before you plan to be there and order the papers over the phone.

☙ Resources Available

Current domestic newspapers are available three to seven days after publication. Current foreign newspapers are available six to eight weeks after publication.

Indexes and directories available:

★ *Chronological Index of Newspapers for the Period 1801–1952 in the Collections of the Library of Congress,* by Paul E. Swigart (Washington, DC: Library of Congress, 1956).

★ *A Check List of American Eighteenth Century Newspapers in the Library of Congress, 1704–1820,* by John Van Ness Ingram (Washington, DC: Library of Congress, 1984).

★ Newspapers received currently in the Library of Congress.

★ *Newspapers in Microform* (Washington, DC: Library of Congress, various years).

★ *Gale Directory of Publications and Broadcast Media* (formerly *The Ayer Directory of Publications.* Detroit: Gale Research, published annually).

★ *American Newspapers, 1821 to 1936* (New York: H.W. Wilson, 1937).

★ *History and Bibliography of American Newspapers, 1690 to 1820,* by Clarence Saunders Brigham (Worcester, MA: American Antiquarian Society, 1974–1975).

★ *The Standard Periodical Directory 1983–84.* 8th rev. ed. (New York: Oxbridge Communications, 1982).

★ *Ulrich's International Periodicals Directory.* 22nd ed. 2 vols. (New York: R. R. Bowker, 1983, published biennially).

Some newspapers on microfilm:

★ *New York Times,* from September 1851

★ *Washington Star,* from 16 December 1852

★ *Washington Post,* from 6 December 1877

CD-ROM products available include:

★ County and City Data Book
★ UMI Newspaper Abstracts

Geography and Map Division (LM-B01)

This division houses the largest and most comprehensive cartographic collection in the world and contains material which can help researchers with problems of geographic location. The Geography and Map Division is located on the basement level of the LM.

Procedure

Bring photo-identification. Sign in at the main desk. The librarian will direct you to the proper finding aid. Once you have identified the materials you need, the librarian will get them for you. Generally it only takes a few minutes to retrieve the files.

☙ Resources Available

There is no single comprehensive catalog of the division's holdings; however, there are card and book catalogs that provide access to various sections of the collection.

Of particular interest to genealogists are the land ownership maps and the nineteenth- and early twentieth-century county atlases. There are many world, national, and regional atlases and gazetteers to aid the researcher in determining changes in name and political divisions or affiliation of cities, towns, or counties (e.g., those in Eastern Europe which have undergone numerous changes).

There are a number of manuscript and printed maps of colonial America, the Revolutionary War, the War of 1812, the Civil War and the wars of the twentieth century. There are 700,000 large-scale fire insurance maps published by the Sanborn Map Company. Sanborn began publishing maps in 1867 and has periodically issued and updated detailed plans of 12,000 American cities and towns. There are ward maps which enable a researcher to determine a ward number for a census search. The collection of county plat books is helpful for research especially in the midwestern and mid-Atlantic states.

John Adams Building "LA"

The facilities of the LA that are of interest to the genealogical researcher are the:

→   Photoduplication Service (Public Service Counter)
→   Hebraic Reading Room
→   African and Middle Eastern Reading Room
→   Asian Division Reading Room
→   Science Reading Room

With the exception of the Photoduplication Service, the reading rooms in the LA are for specialized research. Consult the Reference Librarian in the Local History and Genealogy Reading Room for more information.

Photoduplication Service Public Service Counter

This service can provide reproductions of items in the Library's collections: books, maps, manuscripts, etc. Materials from the Rare Book and Special Collection Division can only be copied by the Photoduplication Service. They also process a number of mail requests to the reading rooms. There is a $10.00 minimum charge, and a delivery date of four to six weeks.

A Selection of Library of Congress Materials Available Through the Family History Library System

Index to Biographies in Local Histories in the Library of Congress (Baltimore, MD: Magna Carta Book Co., [1979]). 31 microfilm reels, 1380344–1380373. Microfilm of original type-

written card index housed in the Local History and Genealogy Room of the Library of Congress. The first roll of film includes a listing of reference sources which have been analyzed in the Library of Congress index to biographies in state and local histories.

Library of Congress. Catalog Division. *American and English Genealogies in the Library of Congress* (Washington, DC: Government Printing Office, 1919). Salt Lake City: Filmed by the Genealogical Society of Utah, 1990. 1 microfilm reel, 0994061.

Library of Congress. *Newspapers in Microform: United States: 1948–1983* (Washington, DC: 1984). Salt Lake City: Filmed by the Genealogical Society of Utah, 1990. 1 microfilm reel, 1145942.

Library of Congress. *Newspapers in Microform: Foreign Countries: 1948–1983* (Washington, DC: 1984). Salt Lake City: Filmed by the Genealogical Society of Utah, 1990. 7 microfiche, 6085887.

Library of Congress. Map Division. *A List of Geographical Atlases in the Library of Congress: with Biographical Notes, Compiled under the Direction of Philip Lee Phillips* (Washington, DC: Filmed by the Library of Congress, 1965). 2 microfilm reels, 0407947–0407948.

Library of Congress. *Census Library Project: National Censuses and Vital Statistics in Europe, 1918–1939: An Annotated Bibliography, with 1940–1948 supplement prepared by Henry J. Dubester* (Detroit: Gale Research Co., 1967). Salt Lake City: Filmed by the Genealogical Society of Utah, 1978. 1 microfilm reel, 1181538.

Kenneth M. Stampp, ed. *Records of Ante-Bellum Southern Plantations from the Revolution Through the Civil War: Series C, Selections from Holdings of the Library of Congress* (Frederick, MD: University Publications of America, 1985). 13 microfilm reels, 1534247–1534259.

Library of Congress Collection of Mormon Diaries. Washington, DC: Filmed by the Library of Congress Photoduplication Service, 1950. 13 reels of microfilm, 0485332–0485344. Collection of transcripts of Mormon journals, diaries, biographies, life sketches, historical sketches of localities, etc. The transcripts (chiefly typewritten) were made in 1936–1937 by the Utah Historical Records Survey, Work Projects Administration, Federal Writers' Project—in St. George, Ogden, Logan, Salt Lake City, Provo and elsewhere in Utah—and list (where applicable) the name and locality of the possessor of the original from which the transcripts were made.

Name Index to the Library of Congress Collection of Mormon Diaries, compiled by the Special Collections Department, Merrill Library, Utah State University. Salt Lake City: Filmed by the Genealogical Society of Utah, 1985. 5 microfiche, 6051303. Name index to each name mentioned in the Mormon diaries held by the Library of Congress.

Chapter 5

National Society, Daughters of the American Revolution (NSDAR)

The National Genealogical Society (NGS)

NATIONAL SOCIETY, DAUGHTERS OF THE AMERICAN REVOLUTION

☞ Location
The DAR complex covers the block bounded by 17th and 18th Streets, NW, and C and D Streets, NW. The entrance is located on D Street, midway between 17th and 18th Streets. The wheel chair entrance is located at 1776 C Street. Ring the bell for admittance.

☎ Phone
202-628-1776
202-879-3252 (fax)

🕐 Hours
8:30 AM–4:00 PM Mon–Fri
Library hours only: 8:45 AM–4:00 PM Mon–Fri; 1:00 PM–5:00 PM Sun
Closed Saturday and on Sunday before federal Monday holidays.
NSDAR holds its annual Continental Congress in mid-April, always the week containing the 19th, and is closed to the public.

♿ Public Transportation and Parking
Although the DAR is accessible via public transportation, it is a seven-block walk from the nearest Metro station, Farragut West, at 17th and I Streets. Several buses go down Constitution Avenue. Call Metro for routes and schedules. Parking facilities are located two blocks north at New York Avenue. *Limited* meter parking is available on the streets around the DAR. Free three-hour parking is available on Constitution Avenue between 9:30 AM and 4:00 PM, but it is difficult to find. The Metropolitan Police Department frequently restricts parking on C and D Streets, NW, without warning. Cars parked along Constitution Avenue and 17th Street after 4:00 PM weekdays will be towed.

→ Public Access
There is a $5.00 fee for non-members to use the library. Enter the DAR building through the D Street door and sign in with the guard, who will give you an ID badge. Wear this badge at all times while you are in the building, and return it to the guard when you leave the building for the day.

→ Photoduplication
Library staff will make copies from library books and materials for $.20 a page. Microfilm copies are $.50 each. Copies of DAR membership applications are $4.00. Additional pages filed with the application will be copied at $.50 a page.

✎ Mail Requests
Orders for photocopies from library materials should include author, title, date of publication and pages needed. A maximum of thirty pages per order can be processed. The current price is $.75 for the first page from each book and $.20 for every page thereafter. Checks should be made payable to the "Treasurer General, NSDAR." All requests should be sent to the following address:

DAR Library
Daughters of the American Revolution
1776 D Street, NW
Washington, DC 20006-5392

For copies of microform materials, mail requests will be honored only if exact references are given for the information desired. Enclose a SASE with your request. Write to:

Seimes Microfilm Center
Daughters of the American Revolution
1776 D Street, NW
Washington, DC 20006-5392

Direct all requests for copies of membership applications to the following office:

Office of the Registrar General
Daughters of the American Revolution
1776 D Street, NW
Washington, DC 20006-5392

The Organizing Secretary General maintains the membership records and files. For requests for addresses and National Numbers of individual DAR members, write to:

Office of the Organizing Secretary General
Daughters of the American Revolution
1776 D Street, NW
Washington, DC 20006-5392

✍ Publications
Numerous publications and supplies are available through the Office of the Corresponding Secretary General, including the following:

Application blanks and work sheets
Bylaws of the National Society
DAR Handbook.
DAR Library Catalog, Volume 2: *State and Local Histories and Records.*
DAR Library Catalog, Volume 3: *Acquisitions, 1985–1991.*
DAR Patriot Index. 3 vols.
Is That Lineage Right?
Is That Service Right?
Meet the DAR.
Lineage Research Kit.

For requests for a publication and supplies price list, write to:

Office of the Corresponding Secretary General
Daughters of the American Revolution
1776 D Street, NW
Washington, DC 20006-5392

→ Food and Beverages
There is a lunch room located in the lower level of the DAR building. Because only drink and snack vending machines are available, it is advisable to bring a lunch. The Interior Department cafeteria is next door. A photo ID and an NSDAR visitors badge will be needed to gain access to the Interior Department facility.

General Information

The National Society of the Daughters of the American Revolution houses genealogical materials accumulated by the Society over nearly a century. These resources are available to researchers in three offices:

→   The DAR Library
→   The Seimes Microfilm Center
→   The Office of the Registrar General

Materials available for research include:

★   State, county, and local histories
★   Census records
★   Tax records
★   Published vital records
★   Cemetery records
★   Family histories
★   Family Bible records
★   *DAR Patriot Index*
★   DAR application papers
★   Biographies
★   Documentation files

DAR Library

The library is located in historic Memorial Continental Hall.

Procedure

Sign in and pay the $5.00 per day use fee at the desk if you are not a member of NSDAR, National Society of the Sons of the American Revolution (NSSAR), or National Society of the Children of the American Revolution (NSCAR). If this is your first visit or if you have not been to the library for some time, pick up the information sheets at the entrance desk.

The card catalog is near the reference desk. It is divided into three sections: family name, author/title, and general/geographic subject. Check here for the library's book holdings and their locations. In addition to the card catalog, the library has a four-hundred drawer analytical card catalog. This provides access to genealogical information contained in thousands of books, including the Genealogical Records Committee (GRC) Reports, county histories, and many other sources.

The book collection is basically divided into two sections, state and family. The state books are arranged in alphabetical order on the open stacks, then subdivided into subject categories such as counties, history, military, and vital records. The family genealogies are arranged in alphabetical order on open stacks. Each book is marked "families" on the spine, with the family name and the author noted below.

This term classification or call-word system of arranging and shelving books is unique to the DAR Library. Books are not marked or arranged according to either the Dewey Decimal Classification Scheme or the Library of Congress system. Please note that the numbers which appear in the published *DAR Library Catalog* are not call numbers and will not directly help you find a book on the DAR Library's shelves.

Submit requests for photocopies at the front desk by filling out the form at the desk and prepaying for the copies. Pick up your copies from the cart near the front desk. On very busy days a copy limit may be imposed, otherwise there are no limits on copying.

❦ Resources Available

The library's holdings encompass all U.S. states from the period of original settlement to the twentieth century. Supporting materials for introductory research, guides to other research centers, and basic information on records of other countries are included in the collection. The collection focus is not limited to materials on the Revolutionary period, although this era does represent an important part of the library's holdings. Subject specialties of the DAR Library include the following:

★ County and local histories. In the late 1800s and early 1900s many local histories were published which include biographical sketches of various community residents. Many of these histories are indexed in the analytical card catalog. New county and local histories are accessioned on a continuing basis.

★ The *DAR Library Catalog,* Volume 2: *State and Local Histories and Records* and Volume 3: *Acquisitions 1985–1991* detail the above holdings.

★ Family histories and genealogies. Among the library's holdings are over 25,000 volumes of family histories and genealogies . Many of these books are unpublished typescripts and research notes donated to the library. The *DAR Library Catalog,* Volume 1: *Family Histories and Genealogies,* and Volume 3: *Acquisitions 1985–1991*, detail this part of the collection.

★ File case (FC) materials. Thousands of files containing unpublished family genealogies, charts, Bible records, record abstracts, etc., are located in the library office. Many of these materials were the supporting documents for DAR application papers. Unfortunately, not all supporting records were preserved. These files grow daily as new materials are donated or acquired.

★ Genealogical Records Committee (GRC) Reports. In the late 1920s DAR members began to preserve previously unpublished genealogical records of every type, including cemetery inscriptions, Bible records, deeds, wills, marriage records, military records, census records, and genealogies. The GRC Reports do not cover every county or state completely or evenly, but they contain a great deal of otherwise hard to find material. There are over 10,000 volumes in the various state GRC sets, with the state of New York alone having nearly 900 volumes. Each year, the library adds over 400 new GRC reports. Be aware that records are bound with the volumes of the state from which they were submitted and not necessarily the state from where the records originated.

EXAMPLE: A Missouri GRC book might contain the old Bible records of the Brown family from Virginia. Thus, "Brown Family Bible Records" in a Missouri GRC book could easily be overlooked if a person was searching for a Brown family in Virginia.

Most of the GRC Reports are indexed in the Analytical Index. In addition, nearly 3,000 microfilm reels of these reports made by the LDS Church in 1970–1972 have been indexed by the following publications: *The Cemetery Record Compendium,* by John and Diane Stemmons (Logan, UT: Everton, 1979)*, The Vital Record Compendium,* by John and Diane Stemmons (Logan, UT: Everton, 1979)*, An Index to Some of the Family Records of the Southern States,* by E. Kay Kirkham (Logan, UT: Everton, 1979), and *An Index to Some of the Bibles and Family Records of the United States,* by E. Kay Kirkham (Logan, UT: Everton, 1984). Copies of these indexes are also available in many genealogical libraries. The NSDAR Library owns the microfilms cited in these indexes, and will provide photocopies if specific index references are given.

A large part of the collection is made up of transcribed or abstracted original records. These include public vital records; county probate, marriage, land, census, and tax records; church records; Bible records; and cemetery inscriptions.

★   Periodicals. A large collection of genealogical and historical periodicals and the major indexes are available.

★   War Records and Rosters. The *DAR Patriot Index* lists the Revolutionary War patriots who have been used by members to join the NSDAR. Each listing includes birth and death dates, name of wife, rank, type of service, and state of service.

★   Work Projects Administration Historical Records Survey Reports. The library has custody of a nearly complete set of the valuable WPA reports produced during the 1930s that survey the records and historical resources of many American counties and cities. These reports can prove invaluable in determining whether a locality maintained certain types of records. Many state and church records are also listed in these volumes.

✎   Mail Requests
The staff does not do research. Concise mail inquiries will receive attention and responses as time permits. A list of local researchers who will research for a fee is available upon request. When writing to a local researcher, be sure to include a SASE with your request.

The Seimes Microfilm Center

The Seimes Microfilm Center houses a collection of records on microfilm and microfiche. It continues to grow through the donations of DAR members throughout the United States.

Procedure
Sign in at the librarian's desk. As you use films, list them in the space across from your name on the sign-in sheet. The librarian will obtain the films for you and will refile them when you are finished. The microfilm center cannot make copies of DAR application papers. These must be obtained through the Registrar General's Office.

❦   Resources Available
The books on microfilm are cataloged on the analytical cards in the main library catalog. Many are rare, out-of-print books. The printed indexes to the federal census records are in the

library, but the actual census schedules are on microfilm in Seimes.

Major Holdings of The Seimes Microfilm Center

General Collection

★   NSDAR Original and Supplemental Application Papers of Members: These papers list each member's descent from a Revolutionary War patriot and the sources of information used to prove both lineage and service. Page two of the application gives the lineage; page three lists the references (often available in the library); and page four relates the patriot's service. Early applications (pre-1930) contain little information other than the names of the applicant's direct ancestors and the patriot's name and service in the Revolution.

★   Federal census records, miscellaneous years, states, and territories. Included are population schedules, veterans' censuses, and soundexes.

★   Mortality schedules 1850–1880 for Arizona, Colorado, the District of Columbia, Georgia, Kansas, Kentucky, Louisiana, Maryland, Michigan, New Jersey, South Carolina, and Tennessee.

★   The Draper Collection of historical records of the Revolution and westward expansion.

★   Hessian documents of the American Revolution, 1776–1783 (mostly in English).

★   Ledgers of payments to U.S. pensioners under Acts of 1818–1858.

★   Military service records of Revolutionary War soldiers, general index to National Archives, RG93 (M860), and state records.

★   The 1992 International Genealogical Index™ of the Church of Jesus Christ of Latter-day Saints.

★   *Papers of the Continental Congress, 1774–1789.*

★   Fourteen rolls of manuscript notes by William Eardeley, which contain alphabetical genealogies of families (mostly eastern, some southern) from the earliest settlement of this country to the early twentieth century.

State Collections

★   **Arkansas**
Original land grants, tract books 1–97.

★   **Connecticut**
Barbour Collection of vital records prior to 1850.
Charles R. Hale Collection of Connecticut Cemetery Records.
Connecticut State Archives: Revolutionary War, Series I, II, and III.
Hartford Times Index.

★   **Delaware**
New Castle County vital records index.

★   **District of Columbia**
The National Intelligencer marriage and death abstracts, 1800–1850.

★   **Florida**
Spanish land grants.

★   **Georgia**
Colonial records.
Miscellaneous records of Jefferson County.

★   **Illinois**
Indexes for county histories, marriages, and a name index to early records.
Public Domain land sales.
Kaskaskia manuscripts, 1708–1816.

★   **Kentucky**
Kentucky county tax records.
John J. Dickey diary.

★ **Louisiana**
The Christian Advocate, 1851–1915.

★ **Maine**
Maine "Old Cemetery Association" records.
1798 Direct Tax Lists for Maine.

★ **Maryland**
Parish records covering the diocese of Washington, DC and Charles, Prince George's, Montgomery, and St. Mary's counties, Maryland.
Maryland State Archives land tax records.
Maryland Provincial Court, land records tract index, 1658–1777.
Maryland General Court of the Western Shore, tract index, 1777–1806.
Maryland Land Office rent rolls, 1639–1777.

★ **Massachusetts**
Massachusetts vital records filmed from the original records, not complete.
Rollin Cooke Collection of compilations of records from western Massachusetts, Connecticut, New York, Rhode Island, and Vermont.
Corbin Manuscript Collection for central and western Massachusetts, 1650–1850.
1798 Direct Tax List for Massachusetts.

★ **Michigan**
1894 state census.

★ **Minnesota**
1885 state census, Dakota County.
1905 state census, Dakota and Dodge counties.

★ **Missouri**
Miscellaneous county records, 1805–1920.

★ **New Jersey**
Department of Defense, alphabetical list of Revolutionary War New Jersey muster rolls and militia lists.
New Jersey Ratables in the American Revolution.

★ **New York**
Vosburg Collection of early New York church records.
New York Wills, 1680–1879.

★ **North Carolina**
Marriage records, 1741–1868, compiled from various original sources.

North Carolina Revolutionary War Army accounts.
North Carolina warrants and surveys, Western Territory (Tennessee).
North Carolina State Archives: Revolutionary War pay vouchers, land grants, wills, tax lists, etc.
North Carolina cemetery card index.

★ **Ohio**
Ohio county history surname index.
Ohio Civil War regimental histories and reunions.
Ohio Revolutionary War bounty land warrants.
Hamilton County deeds and wills.

★ **Oklahoma**
1896 census, Choctaw Nation.

★ **Pennsylvania**
Records of the Comptroller General: military accounts and militia, 1774–1794.
Tax and exoneration lists by county, 1761–1801.
Military abstract card file.
Franklin and Lancaster counties, tax records, 1794–1847.
Chester County deed books, 1688–1786.

★ **Rhode Island**
Rhode Island Revolutionary War Series Index.

★ **South Carolina**
South Carolina combined alphabetical index, 1784–1868.
South Carolina will transcripts, 1782–1868.
South Carolina land plats and index, 1784–1868.
South Carolina State Archives: memorials of seventeenth- and eighteenth-century South Carolina land titles and index to Auditor General Memorials, 1731–1775.

★ **Vermont**
General index to vital records to 1870.

★ **Virginia**
Public Service Claims: indexed records of Revolutionary War claims made by private citizens who provided goods, services and other material aid during the Revolution.
Journals of the House of Burgesses, 1619–1776.
Virginia half-pay and other related Revolutionary War pension application files.
Virginia Land Office patents.

★   **West Virginia**
Smith-Riffe Collection of New River genealogy and local history.
West Virginia county records, vital and probate.

Office of the Registrar General

This office reviews all DAR membership applications and preserves the applications and accompanying documentation for future reference. The staff genealogists do not do genealogical or historical research for the public.

Procedure
All applications are filed by National Number. The Registrar General's Office will assist in locating the National Numbers of descendants of a particular patriot. To obtain a photocopy of an application, provided it is not restricted, you will need to provide the following information to the Office of the Register General:

When name of Revolutionary ancestor is known:

✓   Full name of Revolutionary War ancestor
✓   Date of his birth and death
✓   Name(s) of his wife/wives
✓   State from which he served during the Revolution
✓   Name of his child through whom descent is claimed. If unknown, indicate if you will accept copies through any child listed.

When name of DAR member is known:

✓   Full name of DAR member
✓   Name of her Revolutionary War ancestor. A member may have more than one proven ancestor.
✓   The active member's written permission to copy her application
✓   If possible, the active member's National Number, chapter and state

A Selection of DAR Resources Available Through the Family History Library System

Daughters of the American Revolution. *DAR Library Card File*. Salt Lake City: Filmed by the Genealogical Society of Utah, 1970. 11 microfilm reels, 0544054–0544064.

Daughters of the American Revolution. *Index of the Rolls of Honor in the Lineage Books of the National Society of the Daughters of the American Revolution*. 4 vols. (1916–1940). (Reprinted Baltimore: Genealogical Publishing Co., 1980). Salt Lake City: Filmed by the Genealogical Society of Utah, 1985. 20 microfiche, 6051293.

NATIONAL GENEALOGICAL SOCIETY

The NGS is a membership organization that maintains a library of published and unpublished works relevant to genealogy. The Society, founded in 1903, maintains a library and a library loan service, issues a variety of publications, and strives to improve genealogical skills and education.

☞ Location
The NGS Library is located behind historic Glebe House at 4527 17th Street North, Arlington, VA 22007.

☎ Phone
Glebe: 703-525-0050
Library: 703-841-9065
Fax: 703-525-0052

🕐 Hours
Library: 10:00 AM–4:00 PM Fri and Sat; 10:00 AM–9:00 PM Mon and Wed
Office: 9 AM–5 PM Mon–Fri

♿ Public Transportation and Parking
Free parking is available on the street. Ballston Metro station is several blocks south of NGS. Call Metrobus for routes and schedules for your area.

→ Public Access Policies
Non-members must pay a daily use fee of $5.00.

Food and beverages are not allowed in the library. All bags must be checked at the checkout desk. Only the main level is wheelchair accessible, but staff will obtain materials from other floors upon request.

→ Photoduplication
Self-service photocopying is available for twenty cents a copy.

❖ Online Database Services
E-mail address:
ngs.library@f302n109.z1.fidonet.org

NGS BBS: 703-528-2612
For a detailed explanation of the bulletin board system see *Genealogy Online: Researching Your Roots,* by Elizabeth P. Crowe (New York: Windcrest/McGraw Hill, 1995).

NGS is now online with CompuServe in two forums. The ROOTS forum is a message board. NGS also has a section of GENSUP (Genealogy Support Forum).

NGS has also opened a WWW (World Wide Web) Home Page on Internet at URL: http://genealolgy.org/NGS/

✎ Mail Requests and Services
National Genealogical Society
4527 17th Street North
Arlington, VA 22207

Research is conducted for $15.00 an hour, with a one hour minimum. A check for not more than $65.00 must accompany the query. Photocopies are additional. This is a members-only service.

A home study course, "American Genealogy: A Basic Course," comprised of sixteen lessons, is offered to members and non-members. For information write to the education division at the above address.

✍ Publications
The Society publishes a journal, *NGS Quarterly,* and a bi-monthly newsletter, *NGS Newsletter,* including the *NGS/CIG Digest.* An instructional pamphlet, *Suggestions for Beginners in Genealogy,* is free. A complete list of publications is available by mail or at the library.

Procedure
The library is free to NGS members. Sign in as you enter the library and pay the daily use fee if you are not a member. Volunteer staff members will direct you to the books or records you need.

❦ Resources Available
The Society library contains over 23,000 volumes, including family histories, county histories, transcribed source materials, and reference volumes. Many of these books are available for loan, either by mail or in person, for members only. A Bible record collection and a large number of member ancestral charts are available to members only. There is a variety of miscellaneous material in vertical files.

The library card catalog is on the main floor. The catalog is divided into three sections:

★   General, indexed by subject, title, and author
★   State and local history, indexed by state, county, and city
★   Family history, indexed by surname

Each index card is marked with a Library of Congress call number and the shelf location of the item. An index card with the initials "FC" in place of a call number indicates the item is located in a file cabinet. A member of the library staff will return it to the file when you have finished.

The manuscript files are stored in the Glebe House. This collection is partially cataloged but can only be used by NGS members during hours when the Glebe House is open. Manuscripts will be pulled for viewing in the library at that time.

The library building has three levels, and the collection is organized as follows:

Main level: card catalog, reference materials, history collections, military collections, ship passenger publications, NGS publications, computers, photocopy machines, and a restroom.

Upper level: state and local history, periodicals, microfiche materials and readers.

Lower level: genealogies and family histories, periodicals, historical and genealogical society publications, family society newsletters, file cabinet materials, MAC files (Members' Ancestor Charts), audio collections.

CD-ROM products available
FamilySearch®
PhoneDisc®
New England Historical and Genealogical Register
General Land Office Automated Records

A Selection of NGS Resources Available Through the Family History Library System

The FHL has recently completed filming all of the MAC charts, Bible records, and the Descendants of Illegitimate Sons and Daughters of the Kings of England lineage papers.

National Genealogical Society Genealogical Records: Received Through the National Genealogical Society, Arranged by the Genealogical Society of Salt Lake City, Utah, 1951–1953. Salt Lake City: Filmed by the Genealogical Society of Utah, 1983. 1 microfilm reel, 1035526.

National Genealogical Society Quarterly (Washington, DC: National Genealogical Society, 1912–). Salt Lake City: Filmed by the Genealogical Society of Utah, 1957, 1986. 9 microfilm reels, computer no. 0209748. Most issues include indexes. Volumes 31, 36, 40, 44, and 50 include an index of Revolutionary War pension applications.

Chapter 6
Facilities for Military Records and Research

American Battle Monuments Commission (ABMC)

☞ Location and Mailing Address
Casimir Pulaski Building
20 Massachusetts Avenue, NW
Washington, DC 20314-0300

☎ Phone:
202-761-0537

→ Public Access
The ABMC is open to the public. The staff will search burial information on U.S. servicemen and women buried overseas, and Filipino servicemen and women buried in the Philippines. They will accept mail and phone requests.

✍ Publications
American Memorials and Overseas Military Cemeteries (Washington, DC: American Battle Monuments Commission, 1994) contains information on all cemeteries and maps showing their locations.

❦ Resources Available
The ABMC is a small independent agency of the Executive Branch of the federal government, established by Congress in 1923. It is responsible for operating and maintaining twenty-four permanent American military burial grounds on foreign soil. Its records begin at the date of the U.S. entry into World War I, 6 April 1917.

The ABMC provides a free information service to families and friends of all those who are interred or memorialized in these cemeteries. The information provided includes:

✓ Name
✓ Location of cemetery
✓ Plot, row, and grave number, if appropriate

✓ Suggested routes of travel to reach the cemetery
✓ Information about accommodations
✓ Black and white photographs of headstones, or sections of Tablets of the Missing (those known dead whose bodies have not been recovered).

These records are also available at the National Archives, Record Group (RG) 117.

Department of Defense and Related Sources

Department of the Air Force

Center for Air Force History Library
Bolling Air Force Base
Building 5681
170 Luke Avenue
Washington, DC 20332-6098

☎ Phone
202-767-0412

→ Public Access
The library is open to the public by appointment for on-site research. Phone ahead to secure a pass at the gate to get on base. Staff assistance is available on how to use the facility; researchers must do their own work.

✍ Publications
Morse, Richard. *Personal Papers in the United States Air Force Historical Research Center* (Washington, DC, 1990).

Maryanow, Maurice. *Catalogue of the United States Air Force Oral History Collection* (Washington, DC, 1989).

Guide to the Resources of the United States Air Force Historical Research Center (Montgomery, AL: Maxwell Air Force Base, 1983).

❦ Resources Available
The library's holdings include a microfilm collection of unit histories, histories of specific wars, and oral histories. A catalog is available.

Department of the Army and Other Army Sources

Arlington National Cemetery
Superintendent
Arlington National Cemetery
Arlington, VA 22211

☎ Phone
703-697-2131

→ Public Access
On-site information is available. Phone and mail requests are accepted.

✍ Publications
Arlington National Cemetery (Washington, DC, n.d.).

❦ Resources Available
The staff can provide information on grave and section numbers of all interments and burial records of anyone buried in Arlington National Cemetery. There is a card index on site that staff can search by surname or Social Security number. They can also determine if an individual is eligible for interment in the cemetery.

U.S. Army Engineer Museum
16th Street and Belvoir Road
Building 1000
Ft. Belvoir, VA 22060

☎ Phone
703-664-6104

→ Public Access
The museum is located at Fort Belvoir and is open to the public.

✍ Publications
Schubert, Frank N., ed. *The Nation Builders: A Sesquicentennial History of the Corps of Topographical Engineers* (Fort Belvoir, VA: Office of History, U.S. Army Corps of Engineers, 1988).

RECRUITS, U.S. ARMY, ca. 1918

❦ Resources Available
Library holdings include manuscripts and documents relating to Army Corps of Engineers history. Highlights of the collection are French maps and journals of the siege of Yorktown; correspondence and diaries of members of the Corps; documents relating to Fort Belvoir Plantation; and a photograph and slide collection.

U.S. Army Military History Institute
Carlisle Barracks
Carlisle, PA 17013-5008

☎ Phone
717-245-3611

→ Public Access
The Institute is open to the public for on-site research, but a prior phone consultation is suggested. Photoduplication is available. The staff will make copies from the photographic collection for a fee.

✍ Publications
A Guide to the U.S. Army Military History Institute (Carlisle Barracks, PA: U.S. Army Military History Institute, out of print).

❦ Resources Available
This facility holds the "unofficial" history of the U.S. Army (for the official history, see National Archives RG 111, Entry 108US). It is about a two hour drive from Washington. Holdings can be searched through an online catalog. Items of special interest include:

★ Large microfilm collection
★ 750,000 photographs
★ Collection of Civil War photographs
★ Nineteenth-century newspaper collection
★ Historical material on war
★ Campaign information
★ Unit and regimental histories
★ Unit muster rolls of the Civil War for the Union Army only

The Old Guard Museum
Sheridan Avenue
Building 249
Fort Myer, VA 22211

☎ Phone
703-696-6670

→ Public Access
The museum is open to the public and located at Fort Myer, near Arlington National Cemetery. The Military Police at the gate will direct you to the museum.

✍ Publications
The Old Guard Museum: Traditions and History of the Army's Oldest Unit.

❦ Resources Available
The museum holds the historical collection of the 3rd Infantry, the oldest infantry unit in the United States. Their records of officers and enlisted personnel are compiled from various sources and are of an historic, not official, nature.

National Guard
National Guard Association Library
One Massachusetts Avenue, NW
Washington, DC 20001

☎ Phone
202-789-0031

→ Public Access
Open to the public for on-site research.

❦ Resources Available
The library's holdings are organized on a state by state basis. A catalog is available as a shelf binder and a card index; an online catalog is being compiled. Items of interest to researchers include a collection of regimental histories. The focus of the collection is on the Guard's role as warfighters.

Department of the Navy and Other Naval Sources
Marine Corps Historical Center
Washington Navy Yard
Building 58
9th and M Streets, SE
Washington, DC 20374-0580

☎ Phone
202-433-3483

→ Public Access
The center is open to the public; call ahead.

✍ Published Finding Aids
Guide to the Marine Corps Historical Center.

Resources Available

★ 25,000-volume reference library
★ Unit histories
★ 6,400 oral histories, bound transcripts, and tapes
★ 1,500 manuscript boxes of personal papers
★ Geographic files
★ Biographical files
★ Muster rolls on microfilm
★ Personnel registers of officers from 1800
★ Historical photograph file

Navy Historical Center
Washington Navy Yard
9th and M Streets, SE
Washington, DC 20374-0571

☎ Phone
202-433-2765 Operational Archives
202-433-3170 Curator Branch, Photographic
Section and Ships Histories Branch, Building
108

→ Public Access
Open to the public for on site-use. Call in advance. Photoduplication facilities are available.

✍ Publications
Information for Visitors to the Operational
Archives.
*Declassified Records in the Operational
Archives, Naval Historical Center.*
Allard, Dean C. and Betty Bern. *U.S. Naval
History Sources in the Washington Area, and
Suggested Research Subjects* (Washington, DC:
Naval History Division, 1976).

❦ Operational Archives, Resources Available
The Archives maintains custody of manuscripts
and documents used by the Navy for historical
research. Most of the records before 1950 have
been declassified. Items of special interest
include:

★ War diaries
★ 500 oral histories on tape; also bound
  copies of the Naval Institute's oral
  histories
★ Biographical files of officers
★ Ship and unit historical files
★ Reference materials for the Japanese,
  German, and British navies

❦ Photographic Section and Ships Histories
Branch, Resources Available
The Photographic Section has custody of
250,000 images, including photos and prints of
every Navy ship built between 1800 and 1920.
These photos are available on site for a fee.
There is also a collection of post-1920 materials not found at the National Archives and Department of Defense Still Media Records Center. An online index allows researchers to search
the collection by person, place, event, ship, and
weapon.

The section can provide the negative number
of photos of most later ships between 1920 and
1982. These are located in the Still Picture
Research Room at Archives II in College Park,
MD. Archives II does not provide copies of the
photos but will refer patrons to an approved
vendor.

Photos of ships from 1982 to the present are
obtained through the DOD Still Media Records
Center, described in this chapter.

The Ships Histories Branch has files on every
vessel that has been commissioned in the U.S.
Navy.

Navy Department Library
Washington Navy Yard
Building 44
9th and M Streets, SE
Washington, DC 20374

☎ Phone
202-433-4131

→ Public Access
Open to the public for on-site research. Call
ahead.

✍ Publications
Navy Department Library: A Brief Description.

❦ Resources Available
Holdings include over 170,000 volumes and
over 8,000 reels of microfilm. Items of special
interest include:

★ Newspapers and periodicals from the
  American Revolution on microfilm
★ European naval records, particularly
  Great Britain
★ A larger collection of operational
  records than the Navy Historical
  Center
★ Campaign information
★ Samuel Elliot Morrison's Pacific War
  history manuscripts
★ Ships' registers and data books
★ Cruise books
★ Naval registers and directories
★ Officers' papers
★ Special submarine collection

Navy Memorial
701 Pennsylvania Avenue, NW
Washington, DC

☎ Phone
202-737-2300

→ Public Access
The public is encouraged to visit this memorial.

❦ Resources Available
The Navy Memorial is the showpiece for commemorating all the personnel of the U.S. Navy. There is an online database containing information that has been contributed by former Navy personnel. Total records are about 250,000 and include:

✓ Full name
✓ Dates of service
✓ Rank upon retirement

Naval Military Personnel Command (NMPC)
Assistant for Liaison and Correspondence
Washington, DC 20370

☎ Phone
202-614-3155 (Personnel locator office)

→ Public Access
A valid military ID is required. There is contact by phone and mail only, unless accessing your own personnel record.

❦ Resources Available
Phone inquiries are taken regarding the whereabouts of all active duty enlisted personnel and all officers of the Navy and Marine Corps. Searches are made from an online database. Knowing an individual's Social Security number will expedite the search.

The staff accepts written inquiries as to location of Navy personnel. They will forward a personal letter if an individual can be located. Send the letter in a sealed envelope; enclose the letter to be forwarded in a stamped envelope, ready to be mailed.

Department of the Navy
Office of Public Information
Casualties Assistance Branch
Washington, DC 20320

☎ Phone
800-368-3202
703-614-2926

→ Public Access
A valid military ID is required. Phone and mail inquiries accepted.

❦ Resources Available
The office accepts written and phone requests to check recent deaths. They also have some information on Vietnam War casualties. According to their office, information on World War II casualties is not available.

U.S. Naval Academy Archives
Nimitz Library
589 McNair Road
Annapolis, MD 21402-5033

☎ Phone
410-268-2178

→ Public Access
Open to the public.

✍ Publications
Records of the U.S. Naval Academy: Inventory of Record Group 405 (Washington, DC: National Archives and Records Administration, 1975).

Sweetman, Jack. *The U.S. Naval Academy, An Illustrated History.* 2nd ed., revised by Thomas J. Cutler (Annapolis: USNI, 1995).

❦ Resources Available
Some Academy records have been filmed by the National Archives and are available on site. Biographical jacket files on Academy alumni are also available. Oral histories collected by the Naval Institute are also part of the archives.

United States Naval Institute
118 Maryland Avenue
Annapolis, MD 21402-5035

☎ Phone
410-268-6110

→ Public Access
Open to the public.

✍ Publications
Naval History (published bi-monthly).
Proceedings (published monthly).

❧ Resources Available
The Institute serves as the Navy's professional officers' association. Holdings include more than 450,000 naval and maritime photos, including aircraft, which can be reproduced for a fee. Preview copies are available for twenty cents each. There is also a reunion service to locate former shipmates, and an ongoing oral history program that is being accessioned to the Naval Academy Archives.

Department of Defense

DOD Still Media Records Center
Anacostia Naval Station
Building 168
2701 South Capitol Street, SE
Washington, DC 20374-5000

This agency is scheduled to transfer to March Air Force Base in San Bernadino, CA sometime in 1996. The new mailing address will be: Defense Visual Information Center, Att: Still Media Operations, 1363 Z Street, Bldg. 2730, March Air Force Base, CA 92518-2717. The services should remain the same.

☎ Phone
202-433-2168

→ Public Access
The center is open with restrictions. Appointment required with seventy-two hours' notice. Phone and mail requests are accepted. Orders may be placed by phone, and an invoice will be sent.

❧ Resources Available
The Center is the central repository for all photographic records of the Department of Defense. It holds over one million Armed Forces photographic records. Copies are available for purchase. These photos include all images taken since 1982. Pre-1982 photos are held by the

National Archives Still Picture Branch at Archives II. The notable exception to this policy is Air Force photographs taken before 1954. They are in the custody of the National Air and Space Museum (see chapter 7).

Department of the Interior

National Park Service
Public Inquiries Office
P.O. Box 37127
Washington, DC 20013-7127

☎ Phone
202-619-7222

Area battlefield parks operated by the NPS

Antietam National Battlefield
P.O. Box 58
Sharpsburg, MD 21782
Phone: 301-432-7675

Fredericksburg Battlefield National
Military Park
1013 Lafayette Boulevard
Fredericksburg, VA 22405
Phone: 540-373-6122

Harper's Ferry National Historical Park
P.O. Box 65
Harpers Ferry, WV 25425
Phone: 304-535-6881

Manassas National Battlefield
1251 Lee Highway
Manassas, VA 22110
Phone: 703-754-1861

❧ Resources Available
Each site has an historian to assist with research, but a prior appointment is recommended.

The NPS is placing over five million names into a CD-ROM system called the Civil War Soldiers' System (CWSS). The soldiers in the Park Service data base are being entered by volunteers around the country, in cooperation with the Genealogical Society of Utah, the Federation of Genealogical Societies, the National Archives, and the Civil War Trust. A soldier's record will contain the following information:

✓ Rank in and rank out of the service
✓ Regiment
✓ Battles of the regiment
✓ Battles of the soldier
✓ Photo of the soldier, if available
✓ Photos of the battlefields
✓ Burial information for certain sites

The general index cards at the National Archives contain the bulk of the records that will comprise the database of about three and one-half million soldiers. The United Daughters of the Confederacy (UDC) is working with the NPS to coordinate data entry for all former Confederate states. A pilot version of this system is available at the Antietam Battlefield Park. For more information about the CWSS write to:

FGS Business Office
Civil War Project
P.O. Box 3385
Salt Lake City, UT 84110-3385

Vietnam Veterans Memorial
900 Ohio Drive
Washington, DC 20242

☎ Phone
202-634-1568

Publications
Vietnam Veterans Memorial. *Directory of Names* (Washington, DC: Vietnam Veterans Memorial Fund, n.d.). This index serves as a finding aid to the names on the monument. The panel and line number will pinpoint the location of the name being searched.

Magnet Interactive Studios, a private concern, is producing a multimedia CD-ROM entitled *The Wall: A Living Memorial*. It includes a directory of the 58,000 names that are memorialized on the wall. The information will be the same as on the wall, plus the line and panel number.

❦ Resources Available
As of March 1995, the Vietnam Veterans Memorial has 58,196 names. It was dedicated in March 1982, listing names chronologically, beginning with the first casualty. Also included are 1,300 people that are still missing. Infor-

mation inscribed includes the name, rank, and branch of service.

FHL and FHC Resources Available
The Military Index on CD-ROM, part of the FamilySearch program, is available at all family history centers. It contains most casualty records from the Vietnam and Korean wars.

Department of Transportation
U.S. Coast Guard

Coast Guard Historian's Office
2100 Second Street, SW
Washington, DC 20593

☎ Phone
202-267-0948

→ Public Access
Open to the public for on-site research.

✍ Publications
A Bibliography of Coast Guard History, available by mail upon request.
Noble, Dennis L., comp. *Historical Register, U.S. Revenue Cutter Service Officers, 1790–1914* (Washington, DC: Coast Guard Historian's Office, 1990).

❦ Resources Available
There is a collection of material on officers. Card files are available with personnel information that the staff can access. Holdings include over one million photographs from 1850 to the present; copies are available for a fee.

Department of Veterans Affairs

National Cemetery System
Department of Veterans Affairs
810 Vermont Avenue, NW
Washington, DC 20420

☎ Phone
202-273-5177

→ Public Accesss
The office is open to the public and will do telephone searches.

✍ Publications
Interments in National Cemeteries.

❦ Resources Available
Formerly known as the Veterans Administration or "V.A.," the system oversees and maintains 113 national cemeteries and has custody of over two million burial records. The staff will respond to inquiries on any of the burial records. Written requests should include the following information: person's full name, date and place of birth, date and place of death, state in which the veteran enlisted in the military, and the unit of service while on active duty.

Arlington National Cemetery records are kept by the Department of the Army and cannot be provided by the National Cemetery System.

Library of Congress

See chapter 4

National Archives and Records Administration

See chapter 2 for information on locations and types of record groups held by the NARA.

National Society, Daughters of the American Revolution

See chapter 5

U.S. Government Printing Office

There are a number of free subject bibliographies that can aid in military research. These catalogs each cover a particular area of interest, and list the related books, periodicals, pamphlets, and subscription services available for sale from the Superintendent of Documents. A small selection is listed here:

American Revolution, Subject Bibliography (SB) 144
Armed Forces (SB) 131
Civil War (SB) 192
Coast Guard (SB) 263
Military History (SB) 098
Marine Corps (SB) 237
Naval History (SB) 236

A book, *Guide to United States Army Museums* (Washington, DC: 1992, #008-029-00264-7, $9.00), covers resources available in Army and National Guard museums.

See chapter 7 for more information on the Government Printing Office, ordering information, and location of bookstores in Washington, DC.

Chapter 7
Federal Government Agencies and Public Facilities

Government facilities are not always set up to be user friendly. Phone numbers change frequently, as do the personnel. A general phone number to call for changes and updates is the Federal Information Center, at 1-800-722-9000.

For a detailed description of how to conduct research using the agencies of the federal government, consult *The New York Public Library Book of How and Where to Look It Up*, by Sherwood Harris (New York: Prentice Hall, 1991).

Department of Commerce

Census Bureau Library
Federal Office Building 3
Wing 4, Room 2451
Suitland and Silver Hill Road
Suitland, MD 20233

☎ Phone
301-457-2511

→ Public Access
The library is open to the public.

✍ Publications
Catalogs of the Bureau of the Census Library (Boston: G.K. Hall, 1976). Supplements have been published.

Telephone Contacts for Data Users. January 1995. This includes phone numbers for national, state, and local data centers; also national census information centers.

❦ Resources Available
The library has copies of all Census Bureau reports from 1790 to the present. Items include censuses, yearbooks, and statistical and demographic publications. There is also a collection of historical census photographs. Special items include microfilms of every Latin American and Caribbean census taken between 1950 and 1960; and studies from World War II to the present on international migration.

A daily shuttle runs between the Census Bureau Library and the main Commerce Building in Washington.

Department of Health and Human Services

National Library of Medicine
8600 Rockville Pike
Bethesda, MD 20894

☎ Phone
301-496-6095

→ Public Access
The library is open to the public for on-site use. Stacks are open for employees only. Non-employees may request that materials be delivered to the reading room. First-time researchers must register at the circulation desk.

✍ Publications
Index-Catalog of the Library of the Surgeon General, 1880–1961.
National Library of Medicine Current Catalog, 1965–present.
Index Medicus (journal articles).

❦ Resources Available
This library is part of the Public Health Service at the National Institutes of Health. Total items in the collection number about four million volumes, which includes the 600,000-volume collection of the history of medicine, and

it is the largest collection in the world on biomedical science. The earliest items in the history collection are rare books from the sixteenth and seventeenth centuries on New World, West Indies, and Latin American medicine and health.

An online catalog, CATLINE, is available. There is also a special card catalog for holdings that date prior to 1801, called the Americana collection. The bibliographic database MEDLARS (Medical Literature Analysis and Retrieval System) cites several million references in books and journals. This system is available at over 50,000 sites in the U.S.

Other resources include MEDLINE, BIO-ETHICSLINE, and HISTLINE (see chapter 10 for more information).

Health and Human Services Publications Available Through the Government Printing Office

Where to Write for Vital Records: Births, Deaths, Marriages, and Divorces (Washington, DC, 1993).
Do You Know Which 1990 Census Products Contain Data on Ancestry? (Washington, DC, 1994).

See the GPO Section, this chapter, for ordering information.

Department of the Interior

Bureau of Land Management (Springfield)
See chapter 4

Geological Survey Library (Reston)
See chapter 4

National Park Service
See chapter 6 and chapter 12

National Park Service History Collection
Office of Library
Harpers Ferry Center
Harpers Ferry, WV 25425

☎ Phone
304-535-6491

→ Public Access
The library is open to the public for on-site research, but a prior appointment is required.

❧ Resources Available
The audio-visual collection of the NPS is maintained here. Holdings include over one million items, including photographs and oral histories. The oral history collection includes an Ellis Island collection of interviews.

Department of the Interior Library
C Street between 18th and 19th Streets
Washington, DC 20240

☎ Phone
202-208-5815

→ Public Access
The library is open to the public for on-site research.

❧ Resources Available
Library holdings include:

★ Native American collection
★ Complete set of the *American State Papers*
★ U.S. military history
★ History of the public land survey system
★ U.S. and international periodicals collection

Bureau of Indian Affairs (BIA)
Branch of Tribal Enrollment Services
MS 2611
18th and C Streets, NW
Washington, DC 20240

☎ Phone
202-208-3702

→ Public Access
The branch accepts mail and phone inquiries only. All records are in the custody of the NARA.

✍ Publications
The BIA staff recommends the twenty-volume *Handbook of North American Indians* published by the Smithsonian Institution. It is available from the U.S. Government Printing Office.

❦ Resources Available
The Branch of Tribal Enrollment Services will provide, on request, an ancestry packet, which contains tribal information, NARA information, and the address of the closest family history center (LDS).

Department of State

Foreign Service Institute
National Foreign Affairs Training Center (NFATC)
4000 Arlington Boulevard
Arlington, VA 22204-1500

☎ Phone
703-302-7144 (Registrar's Office)

→ Public Access
The institute is not open to the public, but phone inquiries are accepted.

❦ Resources Available
This center is the State Department training facility. The staff teaches courses in fifty-two languages. Instructors and advanced students can offer translation services on a fee or pro bono basis.

Public Affairs Office and Bureau of Consular Affairs
U.S. Department of State
Washington, DC 20520-4818

☎ Phone
202-647-6575 (general information)
202-647-5225 (Travel Warnings and Consular Information Sheets)
202-647-3000 (fax)

❦ Resources Available
Country Desk Officers are assigned for each country. They can provide information on doctors, local public facilities, education, etc.

The State Department issues Consular Information Sheets for every country in the world. They include such information as the location of the U.S. embassy or consulate, health conditions, political disturbances, currency, crime, and security information.

State also issues Travel Warnings to recommend that Americans avoid travelling to a certain country. Call the above phone number for more information.

For more detailed information on any country, *Background Notes* are brief, factual pamphlets that contain data on culture, geography, history, government, economy, and political conditions. These can be ordered through the GPO, or by calling the general information number above.

Other Publications Available Through the Government Printing Office
Foreign Entry Requirements (Pub # 10254)
Your Trip Abroad
Travel Tips for Older Americans
Foreign Country Studies (SB) 166

Smithsonian Institution

National Air and Space Museum
7th Street and Independence Avenue, SW
Washington, DC 20560

☎ Phone
202-357-2700

→ Public Access
The museum archives are open to adults over eighteen years of age, but advance appointments are required.

✍ Publications
O'Connor, Diane Vogt. *Guide to Photographic Collections at the Smithsonian*. Volumes 1–4 (Washington, DC: Smithsonian Institution, 1989–1994).

❦ Resources Available
Among the holdings of the Photographic Archives is the U.S. Air Force collection of images taken between 1903 and 1954.

National Museum of American History
Archives Center
12th Street and Constitution Avenue, NW
Washington, DC 20560

☎ Phone
202-357-3270

→ Public Access
The facility is open to researchers, but a prior phone consultation is recommended.

✍ Publications
Finding Aid: Guide to the Smithsonian Archives

☙ Resources Available
There are more than 4,000 different research collections in the Archives Center. Some of the topics included are:

★   American history
★   Dwight D. Eisenhower Institute for Historical Research. Military history, wide range of topics, including 5,000 volumes from the American Military Institute
★   Women's history
★   African American culture
★   Civil rights
★   Americana

Woodrow Wilson International Center for Scholars
Smithsonian Institution Building
1000 Jefferson Drive, SW
Washington DC 20560

☎ Phone
202-357-2429

→ Public Access
Open with prior permission of the librarian, and to members.

✍ Publications
The Simmons Russica Collection in the Keenan Institute Library.
Scholars' Guide to Washington, DC.

☙ Resources Available
The Wilson Institute was established by the U.S. Congress in 1968 to promote the use of unique human, archival, and institutional resources in the nation's capital for studies illuminating our understanding of the past and the present.

Holdings include 27,000 volumes of reference works. The Keenan Institute for Advanced Russian Studies is located here. The center also has access to special collections in the Library of Congress and other federal government libraries.

U.S. Government Printing Office

The GPO stocks any government book or publication currently offered for sale. Items can be purchased at U.S. government bookstores by phone, fax, or mail.

☎ Phone
202-512-2250
202-512-1800 (fax)

✎ Mail Order
Superintendent of Documents
P.O. Box 371954
Pittsburgh, PA 15250-7954

✍ Publications
For information on the 12,000 items for sale, or free, request:
United States Government Information Subject Bibliography Index.

❖ Online Database Services
Use DIALOG, DIALORDER feature to access PRF (Publications Reference File), a catalog of over 16,000 publications.

U.S. Government Bookstores in Washington

U.S. Government Printing Office
710 N. Capitol Street, NW
Washington, DC 20401
202-512-1355

U.S. Government Bookstore
1510 H Street, NW
Washington, DC 20005
202-653-5075

Chapter 8
Government and Public Facilities, State, County, Regional, and Local, in Maryland and Virginia

The institutions in Maryland and Virginia are limited to those located in the counties surrounding Washington, DC. Unless otherwise stated, all facilities in this chapter are public and are open for research without restriction.

MARYLAND

State of Maryland

Maryland State Archives
350 Rowe Boulevard
Annapolis, MD 21401

☎ Phone
410-974-3914

🕐 Hours
8:00 AM–4:30 PM Tue-Fri
Sat same hours, except closed from noon–1:00 PM

→ Public Access
Patrons are assigned a desk number with a locker when they arrive. Only pencils, papers, and research materials may be used. Electronic equipment may be used with permission. All copying is done by an in-house service; orders must be placed and paid before 4:00 PM. Same day copying is not always available.

✎ Mail Requests
Research is limited to checking existing indexes for full names or a subject. A list of professional researchers is available by mail. Searches for a $20.00 fee will be undertaken when the following information is provided: full name of person, county of residence, type of information sought, and approximate date of record. Photocopies are additional.

✍ Publications
A Guide to the Index Holdings at the Maryland State Archives (Annapolis, MD: the Archives, 1972, 1988 Appendix).
A Guide to Government Records at the Maryland State Archives (Annapolis, MD: the Archives, 1994).
White, Les. *A Guide to the Microfilm Collection of Newspapers at the Maryland State Archives* (Annapolis, MD: the Archives, 1990).
Jacobsen, Phebe R. *Researching Black Families at the Maryland State Archives* (Annapolis, MD: the Archives, 1984).

❦ Resources Available
The Maryland State Archives is the historical agency and permanent repository for the state of Maryland. It preserves and makes available the public records of state, county, and local government since 1634. Items of interest include:

★ Guides: notebook collection of printed guides on organization and type of holdings
★ Computer resources: name and subject guide for some Maryland court and county materials; special collections; microfilm, maps, plats; census indexes; Maryland State Papers; and more.
★ Card/volume indexes for the following records in the search room: probate records from 1634; marriage, birth, and death records; freedom records; naturalization; census/city directories; military and related service; land office; admiralty, Provincial Court, General Court, and Court of Appeals; Chancery Court;

tax lists; county municipal records; state records; special collections.

★   Newspapers on microfilm
★   Maps and plats including Sanborn Fire Insurance Maps
★   Quaker records, extensive collection
★   German church records
★   Anglican records
★   Vietnam War materials
★   Registers of the Roman Catholic Archdiocese of Baltimore on microfilm
★   District of Columbia records

Some Maryland State Archives Resources Available Through the Family History Library System

Papenfuse, Edward C., Susan A. Collins, and Christopher N. Allan. *A Guide to the Maryland Hall of Records: Local, Judicial and Administrative Records on Microform* (Annapolis: Archives Division, Hall of Records Commission, 1978). Includes: Vol. 1, Allegany through Baltimore counties, including Baltimore City. Salt Lake City: Filmed by the Genealogical Society of Utah, 1990. 3 microfiche, 6049468.

Mead, Elizabeth W., Emil Fossan, and Roger Thomas, eds. *Calendar of Maryland State Papers: No. 1. The Black Books* (Baltimore: Genealogical Publishing Co., 1967). Originally published Annapolis: Hall of Records Commission, 1943. Salt Lake City: Filmed by the Genealogical Society of Utah, 1990. 4 microfiche, 6050087.

Radoff, Morris Leon. *The County Courthouses and Records of Maryland, Part One: The Courthouses* (Annapolis: Hall of Records Commission, 1960). Salt Lake City: Filmed by the Genealogical Society of Utah, 1985. 3 microfiche, 6054101.

Radoff, Morris Leon, Gust Skordas, and Phebe R. Jacobsen. *The County Courthouses and Records of Maryland, Part Two: The Records* (Annapolis: Hall of Records Commission, 1963). Salt Lake City: Filmed by the Genealogical Society of Utah, 1985. 3 microfiche, 6054101.

Patents Series of the Maryland Land Office [1636-1852]. Salt Lake City: Filmed by the Genealogical Society of Utah, 1947. 81 microfilm reels, 0013063–0013140.

Maryland State Law Library
Court of Appeals Building
361 Rowe Boulevard
Annapolis MD 21401

☎ Phone
410-974-3395
410-974-2063 Fax

🕐 Hours
8:30 AM–4:30 PM Mon, Wed, Fri
8:30 AM–9:00 PM Tue, Thu
9:00 AM–4:00 PM Sat

Ⓐ Parking
Limited free parking is available in J lot directly in front of the Court of Appeals Building. Parking for a fee is available at the Naval Academy Stadium lot.

→ Public Access
Reference assistance provided on site and by phone. Materials do not circulate.

✍ Publications
Sources of Basic Genealogical Research in the Maryland State Law Library: A Sampler (Annapolis, MD: the Library, 1988).

❦ Resources Available
The Maryland State Law Library was established in 1826. It serves as a major law and social sciences research library, with a collection of over 240,00 volumes. A significant portion of the collection consists of Marylandia and genealogical reference. CD-ROM products are available, including the Government Publication Index. Subject specialties include:

★   Marylandia and Maryland history
★   Microfilmed editions of Maryland newspapers dating to 1837, and a limited edition of bound copies of these newspapers
★   Selected depository for U.S. government documents
★   Famous Maryland women
★   Chesapeake Bay collection

Holdings also include historical and genealogical collections for Delaware, Georgia, Kentucky, New Hampshire, Pennsylvania, Rhode Island, South Carolina, Virginia, and Vermont.

Maryland Commission on African American History and Culture

Banneker-Douglass Museum
of African American Life and History
84 Franklin Street
Annapolis, MD 21401

☎ Phone
410-974-2893

❦ Resources Available

★ Videos on the civil rights movement
★ Books on African American history in Maryland
★ Books of runaway slave advertisements, listing names of slaves

County Resources

Anne Arundel County

Anne Arundel County Public Library
1410 West Street
Annapolis, MD 21401

☎ Phone
410-222-1750

❦ Resources Available
The genealogy and local history collection is available in the Maryland Room.

Charles County

Charles County Public Library
Charles and Garrett Streets
P.O. Box 490
La Plata, MD 20646

☎ Phone
301-934-9001

❦ Resources Available
Collection materials include materials on Marylandia and southern Maryland.

Charles County Community College
Southern Maryland Studies Center
Mitchell Road
P.O. Box 110
La Plata, MD 20646-0910

☎ Phone
301-934-2251, ext. 610

❦ Resources Available
The collection focus is on southern Maryland counties. Subject specialties include:

★ Accokeek Foundation records
★ Charlotte Hall School Foundation collection file
★ Southern Maryland Room vertical file index
★ Southern Maryland Collection: newspapers on microfilm

Frederick County

C. Burr Artz Library
Maryland Room
110 East Patrick Street
Frederick, MD 21701

☎ Phone
301-631-3764 (Maryland Room)

Publications
Local History and Genealogy Handbook.

❦ Resources Available
Holdings include a large collection of local history and genealogical materials on Maryland. CD-ROM resources include the *New York Times* and *Washington Post* indexes.

Howard County

Howard County Public Library
9421 Frederick Road
Ellicott City, MD 21042

☎ Phone
410-313-1950

❦ Resources Available
This library has a special collection on medicine and medical research. Online catalog and database services are available, including MEDLINE. CD-ROM products include newspaper abstracts and census data.

Montgomery County

Rockville Regional Library
99 Maryland Avenue
Rockville, MD 20850

☎ Phone
301-217-4636

❦ Resources Available
Collection of state and Montgomery County
records. Other holdings include:

★   CD-ROM: *New York Times* and
     Washington Post index
★   Maryland Microcat
★   *Washington Star* newspaper on
     microfilm, 1852–1981

Prince George's County

Prince George's County Memorial Library
Maryland Room
6530 Adelphi Road
Hyattsville, MD 20782

☎ Phone
301-779-9330

❦ Resources Available
Holdings include genealogy and local history
and an African American collection.

Wicomico County

Wicomico County Free Library
Maryland Room
122 South Division Street
Salisbury, MD 21801

☎ Phone
410-749-5171

✍ Publications
*The Genealogy Collection at the Wicomico
County Free Library* (Salisbury, MD: the Li-
brary, n.d.).

❦ Resources Available
An online catalog, LAPCAT, is available. The
library's holdings include:

★   Maryland history
★   Collections on Delaware, North
     Carolina, Ohio, Pennsylvania, South
     Carolina, and Virginia.
★   Microfilm collection
★   Reference collection of genealogy
     "how-to" books
★   Six video presentations of instruction
     on research principles and three on
     African American research
★   Family research files
★   Map case
★   Vertical file of Bible records, group
     sheets, etc.

VIRGINIA

Commonwealth of Virginia

Virginia State Library and Archives
11th Street and Capitol Square
Richmond, VA 23219-3491

☎ Phone
804-786-2306

✤ Online Access and Database Services
Home page http://www.vsla.edu

✍ Publications
*Guide to Genealogical Notes and Charts in the
Archives Branch, Virginia State Library* (Rich-
mond, VA: the Library, 1985).
*Guide to Bible Records in the Archives Branch,
Virginia State Library* (Richmond, VA: the Li-
brary, 1985).
*Guide to the Church Records in the Archives
Branch, Virginia State Library* (Richmond, VA:
the Library, 1985).
Write for current publications list.

❦ Resources Available
Although outside of the national capitol area,
anyone researching in Virginia should be aware
of the vast holdings of this library.

Holdings include over one million items including 49,000 cubic feet of Virginia state, local,
and genealogical records. An online catalog is
available. Please consult the library's publications for more information.

Some Virginia State Library Resources Available Through the Family History Library System

Confederate Pension Applications, Virginia, Acts of 1888, 1900, 1902; Index, 1888–1934. Salt Lake City: Filmed by the Genealogical Society of Utah, 1988. 219 microfilm reels, Computer No. 0534241. Microreproduction of original records at the Virginia State Library and Archives in Richmond, VA.

Virginia State Library. Department of Archives and History. *List of the Revolutionary Soldiers of Virginia.* Special Report of the Department of Archives and History for 1911 and 1912, by H. J. Eckenrode. Salt Lake City: Filmed by the Genealogical Society of Utah, 1954. 1 microfilm reel, 0029893.

Hummel, Ray Orvin. *A List of Places Included in 19th Century Virginia Directories* (Richmond, VA: Virginia State Library, 1960). Salt Lake City: Filmed by the Genealogical Society of Utah, 1984. 1 microfiche, 6019960.

Nugent, Nell Marion. *Cavaliers and Pioneers: Abstracts of Virginia Land Patents and Grants.* Supplement, Northern Neck Grants, no. 1, 1690–1692, abstracted by Nell Marion Nugent; indexed by Susan Bracey Sheppard. 3 vols. (Richmond, VA: Virginia State Library, 1934–1979). Salt Lake City: Filmed by the Genealogical Society of Utah, 1991. 1 fiche, 6050913.

Virginia State Library. *Genealogical Notes* [Collection]. Salt Lake City: Filmed by the Genealogical Society of Utah, 1979. 7 microfilm reels, 0029883–0029889.

Gunston Hall Library
Gunston Hall Plantation
10709 Gunston Road
Mason Neck, VA 22079-3901

☎ Phone
703-550-9220
703-550-9480
e-mail: abaker2@loe.vsla.eeu

→ Public Access
The library is open to the public by appointment; telephone requests are accepted.

☙ Resources Available
Owned by the Commonwealth and administered by the Society of Colonial Dames, the library centers on George Mason and his family. The collection totals over 12,000 volumes and periodicals. Other subject specialties are:

★ Virginia history
★ Eighteenth-century decorative arts
★ The Pamela Copeland Collection of 400 volumes of eighteenth-century genealogy and Americana
★ The Mason family papers and records
★ Microfilm collection, including early Maryland and Virginia newspapers, county records, farm papers, and other records
★ Rare book collection which spans every facet of human life and thought from the fifteenth to the early nineteenth centuries
★ Original newspapers and indentures
★ Gunston Hall school records

County Resources
Arlington County
Arlington County Public Library
Virginia Room
1015 North Quincy Street
Arlington, VA 22201

☎ Phone
703-358-5966

→ Public Access
A valid ID is required. No bags, briefcases, or pens are allowed in the Virginia Room. Appointments are required to use the archives and oral histories.

☙ Resources Available
Virginia Room holdings include books, directories, vertical files, newspapers on microfilm, census records, court records, photographs, and oral history interviews.

Culpeper County
Culpeper Town and County Library
Genealogy Room
105 East Mason Street
Culpeper, VA 22701

☎ Phone
703-825-8691

❦ Resources Available
Library holdings include:

★ Family histories and manuscripts
★ Culpeper newspapers on microfilm from mid-1800s to the present
★ Deeds and wills
★ WPA report on private family cemeteries in the area

Fairfax County

Fairfax City Regional Library
Virginia Room
3915 Chain Bridge Road
Fairfax, VA 22030

☎ Phone
703-246-2123

→ Public Access
Most books are reference books and do not circulate, but there is a small collection that can be checked out.

✎ Mail requests
The staff does minimal research; queries are answered by staff and volunteers. Send short, concise requests with an SASE.

✣ Online Services
You may access the Fairfax County Public Library Online Catalog from a home computer with a modem by dialing the library's dialup access number: 703-802-7447. Once connected, press enter and the prompt MPE XL: should appear. At the prompt, type: HELLO DIALUP.PUBLIC and press enter. Use HE (help) for further instructions.

❦ Resources available
Holdings include a strong collection of local history and genealogy. The collection includes historical and genealogical materials and records for Virginia, Maryland, West Virginia, and Delaware counties; and state and regional materials for New York, Pennsylvania, Ohio, North Carolina, South Carolina, Kentucky, and Tennessee. There is a vertical file of family his-

tories and inquiries, a map collection, and a photographic archive. Holdings include:

★ Fairfax County court records
★ Northern Neck land grants
★ Local newspapers on microfilm
★ Fairfax County cemetery index
★ *Virginia Historical Index,* by E.G. Swem
★ Civil War collection
★ *Official Records of the Union and Confederate Armies in the War of the Rebellion.* 128 volumes (Washington, DC, 1901)
★ NEHGS *Index* and *Register*

Fairfax County Publications Center
1200 Government Center Parkway
Fairfax, VA 22035-0063

☎ Phone
703-324-3187 (public affairs)

❦ Resources Available
Materials available for sale include reasonably priced maps, books, and booklets on local history and Virginiana.

Loudon County

Thomas Balch Public Library
208 West Market Street
Leesburg, VA 22075

☎ Phone
703-777-0132

✍ Publications
Invest in Your Future: Preserve Your Past An Introduction to the Thomas Balch Library.

❦ Resources Available
When the Thomas Balch Library was dedicated in 1921 there was a stipulation that it must maintain a section dedicated to Virginia and Loudon County history. The library is now entirely devoted to genealogy and history. An online catalog is available. Charts and forms are available for purchase.

Prince William County

Bull Run Regional Library
Ruth Emerson Lloyd Information Center
(RELIC)
Virginia Collection
8051 Ashton Avenue
Manassas, VA 22111

☎ Phone
703-792-4500

✍ Publications
Climbing Your Family Tree, A Pathfinder
(Manassas, VA: the Library, 1989).
Prince William County: A Guide to Sources
(Manassas, VA: the Library, 1989).

❦ Resources Available
Bull Run Library is actively supported by the
Prince William County Genealogical Society,
which lists new library accessions to RELIC in
their newsletter, *Kindred Spirits*. Holdings
include:

★　Virginiana
★　Local and regional history and
　　genealogy
★　Civil War collection, including
　　*Official Records of the Union and
　　Confederate Armies in the War of the
　　Rebellion*
★　Microfilm of old Prince William
　　County newspapers
★　CD-ROM collection of 100 discs,
　　including FamilySearch®

Independent Cities

City of Alexandria

Alexandria Public Library
Lloyd House Branch
220 N. Washington Street
Alexandria, VA 22314

☎ Phone
703-838-4577

✍ Publications
Miller's Guide and *Update to Miller's Guide*,
indexes to the vertical file.

❦ Resources Available
The collection includes books, photographs,
maps, microform, periodicals, and manuscripts
pertaining to Alexandria. General genealogical
materials are available for history of the region, Virginia, and the southeastern states, including Virginia and southern genealogies and
history. Some holdings, however, have been
deaccessioned. The focus of the collection is
now mainly Virginia. Holdings include:

★　Civil War collection of 1500 books,
　　including *Official Records of the
　　Union and Confederate Armies in the
　　War of the Rebellion*
★　1,000 genealogies and family
　　histories
★　*Virginia Historical Index,* by E.G.
　　Swem
★　Alexandria and Fairfax County
　　newspapers from 1784 on microfilm
★　*New York Times,* 1861–1865 on
　　microfilm
★　The Lyman Draper Collection on
　　microfilm
★　PERSI indexes to genealogical
　　magazines

Alexandria Black History
Resource Center
Watson Reading Room
638 North Alfred Street
Alexandria, VA 22314

☎ Phone
703-838-4356

❦ Resources Available
A new research library dedicated in October
1995; holdings include a general collection of
historical and cultural materials on African
Americans. Special collections include a vertical file collection on Alexandria. An online
catalog accesses the Alexandria Public Library
System.

City of Fredericksburg

Central Rappahannock Regional Library
Virginiana Room
1201 Caroline Street
Fredericksburg, VA 22401

☎ Phone
540-372-1144

❧ Resources Available
Holdings include, but are not limited to:

★ Microform newspaper collection from the 1770s to the present
★ Surname and obituary indexes
★ Census records of city and local counties on microfilm
★ Vital statistics of city and local counties from mid 1800s to 1920
★ Land deeds on microfilm
★ Caroline County personal property tax records
★ Sanborn Fire Insurance Maps, 1886–1900
★ City of Fredericksburg, city council minutes

City of Winchester

Handley Public Library
Archives Room
Corner of Braddock and Piccadilly Streets
P.O. Box 58
Winchester, VA 22604

☎ Phone
540-662-9041

❧ Resources Available
Holdings include manuscripts, maps, photographs, books on local history and genealogy. Subject specialties include:

★ Shenandoah Valley
★ Civil War
★ Frederick County
★ Archives of the Frederick County Historical Society

Chapter 9
Genealogical Sources for the District of Columbia

Introduction

The District of Columbia came into existence in 1790, formed from lands in Maryland and Virginia. Montgomery County, MD and Fairfax County, VA (including the city of Alexandria), both ceded land to the newly created District. The federal government took up residence in 1800, and the city of Washington was incorporated in 1802. During the War of 1812, most of the public records and buildings were burned, including the Library of Congress.

Virginia's ceded land was returned in 1846. By 1870, the population of Washington had doubled. In 1895 Georgetown was merged into the city of Washington. At this time the boundaries of the city and the District became one and the same.

Records for the District of Columbia are divided among District agencies, the National Archives, the Virginia State Library and Archives, the Maryland State Archives, the city of Alexandria, Virginia, and Montgomery and Prince George's counties in Maryland.

National Archives and Records Administration, Archives I

Also see chapter 2

DC Government Employees Records. RG 351

The following are part of Record Group 351: *Registers of Appointments to Metropolitan Police Force, 1861–1930*, and *Metropolitan Police Service Records, 1861–1930*.

Records in the Orphans Court, Washington County, District of Columbia, 1801–1811. RG 21, M2011

The originals are unbound. There are copies of the 1801 to 1811 records which are in a bound volume. The records are indexed and will usually show the following information: name and age of apprentice, name of one parent, name and trade of master, terms of apprenticeship. There are loose papers dating to 1893.

Divorce Dockets. RG 21
The old divorce docket, 1803 to 1848, is bound in four volumes.

Land and Property. RG 351
The following land and property records are in record group 351:

★ Original deed books, 1792–1869. These include slave manumissions before 1821.
★ Building permits (M1116), 1877–1949
★ Assessment books, 1814–1940
★ Tax books, 1824–1879

The original handwritten deed books are part of Record Group 351. These volumes are in very poor condition, and there is no index at the National Archives. Unless it is absolutely necessary to see the original deed, use the transcripts at the Recorder of Deeds.

Militia Records. RG 94
These contain the registers of militia officers of the District, 1813–1830. The service and pension records for the District of Columbia Union Army, M538, are available here.

Army Old Soldiers Home. RG 231
These records are from 1852–1941 and include date of death of residents of the home. They have been transferred to the Regional Archives in Philadelphia.

EARLY PLAN OF THE CITY OF WASHINGTON, WITH GEORGETOWN APPEARING AT UPPER LEFT. *From Tobias Lear's* Observations on the River Potomac *(1793).*

Police Censuses. RG 351
Police censuses were taken between 1885 and 1925 at irregular intervals. They can be found in *Annual Reports of the Commissioner of the District of Columbia*. These have also been transferred to Philadelphia.

Probate Records. RG 21
Archives I has some nineteenth-century probate administrations and guardianship papers. These are not filmed.

Slavery and Freedmen's Records
There are several groups that contain information for researching slavery, freedmen, emancipations, and manumissions:

★ *Board of Commissioners for Emancipation of Slaves in the District of Columbia, 1862–1863.* RG 217, M520.

★ *Records of the U.S. District Court for the District of Columbia Relating to Slaves, 1851–1863* RG21, M433. Emancipation papers, 1862–1863, manumission papers, 1857–1863, and fugitive slave case papers are in these records.

★ *Habeas Corpus Case Records, 1820–1863, of the U.S. Circuit Court for the District of Columbia.* RG21, M434. These include case records of runaway slaves.

★ *Register of Signatures of Depositors in Branches of the Freedman's Savings and Trust Company,1865–1874.* RG 101, M816.

★ *Index to Deposit Ledgers in Branches of the Freedman's Savings and Trust, 1865–1874.* RG101, M817.

★ U.S. census records, non-population schedules are in RG 29:
Slave Schedules, 1850, M432, roll 57.
Slave Schedules, 1860, M653, roll 105.

Tax Records. RG 351
Some tax records have been microfilmed. They include miscellaneous years in the 1800s for city of Washington assessments, Washington County Levy Court assessment books, tax lists, and general assessment books, and city of Washington assessment lists. There are also tax books for Georgetown, M605. Internal Revenue Lists are in RG58, M760.

Cemetery Records

Also see chapter 10 (Georgetown University and Howard University) and NSDAR, this chapter

Rock Creek Cemetery
Rock Creek Church Road and Webster Streets, NW
Washington, DC 20011

☎ Phone: 202-829-0585

Congressional Cemetery
1801 E Street, SE
Washington, DC 20003

☎ Phone: 202-543-0539

Mount Olivet Cemetery
1300 Bladensburg Road, NE
Washington, DC 20002

☎ Phone: 202-399-3000

Glenwood Cemetery
2219 Lincoln Road, NE
Washington, DC 20002

☎ Phone: 202-667-1016

Arlington National Cemetery
See chapter 6

The Oak Hill Cemetery
3001 R Street, NW
Washington, DC 20007

☎ Phone: 202-337-2835

Prospect Hill Cemetery
2201 North Capitol Street, NE
Washington, DC 20002

☎ Phone: 202-667-0676

> **CLOSE-UP:** Prospect Hill Cemetery is a non-profit, donor driven cemetery, founded by the Concordia Lutheran Church in 1858. It has over 14,000 burials. The cemetery is also the repository and source for burial records, available on site in a card file, on microfilm (1860–1960s), and an online database.
>
> Seventy-five percent of those buried are German immigrants and their families, mostly builders, artisans, tradesmen, dressmakers, and tailors. The history of the cemetery is published in *The Immigrants and Their Cemetery: The Story of Prospect Hill,* by Paul Gleis, available for purchase by writing to Dennis Olson, Administrator, at the above address.

Church Archives

For an inventory of church records in the Washington, DC area, please consult *A Directory of Churches and Religious Organizations in the District of Columbia, 1939* (Washington, DC: District of Columbia Historical Records Survey, 1939), and *Inventory of the Church Archives in the District of Columbia: The Protestant Episcopal Church, Diocese of Washington,* 2 vols. (Washington, DC: Historical Records Survey, 1940).

Episcopal Diocese of Washington
Washington National Cathedral
Mount Saint Alban, NW
Washington, DC 20016-5098

☎ Phone
202-537-6555

❦ Resources Available
The Diocese has twentieth-century parish lists
not found elsewhere. Transcribed records for
many area churches are in the Genealogical
Records Committee (GRC) volumes for the
District of Columbia, at the DAR Library.

Archdiocese of Washington (Roman Catholic)
5001 Eastern Avenue
Hyatsville, MD 20017-0260

☎ Phone
301-853-3800

Holy Trinity Catholic Church records are in the
Special Collections Division of the Melvin
Gelman Library at Georgetown University (see
chapter 10).

City Directories

Directories for the District of Columbia and
Georgetown can be found at Archives I, George
Washington University, the Historical Society
of Washington, the Library of Congress, and
the Martin Luther King Memorial Library.

Clerk of The U.S. District Court

Superior Court for the District of Columbia
Clerk, District of Columbia Superior Court
500 Indiana Avenue, NW
Washington, DC 20001

☎ Phone
202-879-4840 (Marriage License Bureau)
202-879-1499 (Register of Wills, Probate
Division)

❦ Resources Available, Marriage License
   Bureau
The Clerk of the District of Columbia Superior
Court has custody of all marriage records from
1811 to the present. The marriage volumes have
been microfilmed and are available for searching.

There is no consolidated index for public use;
however, each volume contains its own index.

Marriages and deaths, as reported in the *National Intelligencer*, 1800 to 1820, have been
abstracted and microfilmed along with a complete name index. These three rolls of microfilm are located at the National Genealogical
Society in Arlington, VA.

Records for divorce proceedings prior to 1956
are kept here. Divorce documents filed since
1956 are held by the Family Division of this
court, at the same address.

❦ Resources Available, Register of Wills
The Register of Wills has custody of all wills
from February 1801 to the present and maintains a card index to all records. Although the
1801 to 1878 administration and guardianship
records appear in the index, the files are not
located in the courthouse. They have been transferred to Archives I and must be viewed there.

District of Columbia Department of Health and Human Services

Vital Records Branch
Room 3009
425 I Street, NW
Washington, DC 20001

☎ Phone
202-727-9281

❦ Resources Available
The Bureau of Vital Statistics has custody of
birth records from 1871 to the present and death
records from 1855 to the present (except for
1861 and 1862). Copies are $12.00 each.

District of Columbia Public Library

Martin Luther King Memorial Library
Washingtoniana Division
901 G Street, NW
Washington, DC 20001

☎ Phone
202-727-1213

☙ Resources Available

★ DC city directories beginning in 1822
★ DC assessment and real estate directories
★ Biographical sketches and obituary notices of Washington residents
★ Microfilm of all major daily newspapers published in DC since 1800, with partial indexes for the *Washington Star* and *Washington Post*
★ Photographic collection
★ Maps and archival materials from DC organizations and neighborhood groups
★ Oral history research center
★ Working morgue and photo library of the defunct *Washington Star* newspaper published from 1852–1981, which is full of materials for the study of Washington and its families, including clippings arranged by subject
★ U.S. censuses of Washington, DC

District of Columbia, Recorder of Deeds

441 4th Street, NW
Washington, DC 20001

☎ Phone
202-727-5374

☙ Records available
The Recorder of Deeds has custody of all real estate records and land titles from 1792 to the present. There is a general index to all deeds; however, the original 1792 to 1869 deed books are no longer maintained here. This office has only the WPA type-written deed copies for these years. The originals are at Archives I and in poor condition.

An abstract of early land records, by Suzanne Hilton, "The First Landowners of Washington, DC" (*Heritage Quest*, Volume 55, pp.67–79), lists the names of owners of the original lots that were auctioned by the federal government. The records are abstracted from *The Washington Advertiser* for the years 1804–1806. These issues are available on microfilm.

Historical Society of Washington, DC Library

1307 New Hampshire Avenue, NW
Washington, DC 20036-1507

☎ Phone
202-785-2068

→ Public Access
Open to the public.

✍ Publications
The Columbia Historical Society Guide to Research Collections (Washington, DC: the Society, 1984).
Records of the Columbia Historical Society (Washington, DC: the Society, 1897–).

☙ Resources Available
The Society was established as the Columbia Historical Society in 1894. Their resources include:

★ Over 300 historical maps
★ Photograph collection including over 70,000 prints, glass plates, and lantern slides
★ The Thomas G. Machen Print Collection
★ Manuscript collection of over 500 separate collections, including funeral home records
★ Vertical files of cataloged newspaper clippings
★ Records of the Association of the Oldest Inhabitants of the District of Columbia, founded in 1865
★ Washington city directories

Maryland State Archives

Also see chapter 8

District Censuses
Besides federal census enumerations, records exist for District censuses, beginning in 1803. The censuses taken in 1867 and 1878 provide name, age, sex, marital status, color, length of residence, occupation, and country of origin of parents. These can be found at the Maryland State Archives.

National Society, Daughters of the American Revolution

Also see chapter 5

The DAR Library has transcriptions of early marriage records from 1811–1858. A transcribed manuscript collection of Bible records, church records, deaths, marriages, obituaries, and wills for the District is also available. There are also records and transcriptions for the following cemeteries: Rock Creek, Congressional, Holmead, Oak Hill, Glenwood, Queen's Chapel, Methodist, and Old Presbyterian.

U.S. Government Printing Office

See chapter 7 for ordering information

Publications on the District of Columbia include:

Collins, Kathleen. *Washingtoniana Photographs: Collections in the Prints and Photographs Division of the Library of Congress* (Washington, DC, 1989).
Washington, DC: A Traveler's Guide to the District of Columbia and Nearby Attractions (Washington, DC,1989).

Virginia State Library and Archives

Also see chapter 8

The Virginia State Library has Circuit Court order books, 1801–1827, and minute books, 1825–1846. It also has custody of the U.S. District Court minute books, 1801–1825.

A Selection of District of Columbia Resources Available Through the Family History Library System

United States. Bureau of Refugees, Freedmen, and Abandoned Lands. *Records of the Assistant Commissioner for the District of Columbia: 1865–1869*. Washington, DC: National Archives, 1978. 21 microfilm reels, 1605536–1605556 (NARA microfilm publication M843).

"The Bureau of Refugees, Freedmen, and Abandoned Lands, often referred to as the Freedmen's Bureau, was established in the War Department by an act of March 3, 1865. Congress assigned to the Bureau responsibilities that previously had been shared by military commanders and by agents of the Treasury Department. The duties included supervision of all affairs relating to refugees, freedmen, and the custody of abandoned lands and property." —National Archives descriptive pamphlet (DP) M843.

District of Columbia. Recorder of Deeds. *Land Records, 1792–1886; General Index to Deeds, 1792–1919*. Salt Lake City: Filmed by the Genealogical Society of Utah, 1972. 694 microfilm reels, 0875710–0912691.

Congressional Cemetery Association . *Cemetery Records, 1820–1988*. College Park, MD: Howell Microfilm, 1978, 1988; Salt Lake City: Filmed by the Genealogical Society of Utah. 13 microfilm reels, computer no. 0005005. Includes index which covers to 1988. The index is not complete and there are some duplicates and misfilings.

National Intelligencer: Selected Pages, 30 May 1861–16 December 1864. Urbana, IL: University of Illinois Library, 1960. 1 microfilm reel, 0226231, item 2.

United States. Bureau of Refugees, Freedmen, and Abandoned Lands. *Records of the Superintendent of Education for the District of Columbia, Bureau of Refugees, Freedmen and Abandoned Lands, 1865–1872*. Washington, DC: National Archives, 1977. 24 microfilm reels, 1617650–1617673 (NARA microfilm publication M1056).

United States. Adjutant General's Office. *Index to Compiled Service Records of Volunteer Union Soldiers Who Served in Organizations from the District of Columbia*. Washington, DC: National Archives, 1964. 3 microfilm reels, 0881964–0881966 (NARA microfilm publication M538).

Chapter 10
Academic Institutions and Private Archives and Libraries with Genealogical Resources

ACADEMIC INSTITUTIONS

Most colleges, seminaries, and universities do not have an established "genealogical collection," per se, because their holdings are not arranged for this type of research. This does not mean that the resources are not there. They just take more time to identify.

When visiting, rather than ask for genealogical materials, ask how to use the catalog, and where the different collections are physically located. The catalog may be online, or in a card file. Types of searches that will produce useful material:

✓   First: search the locality. Do not search by surname, but browse the catalog under the place names where the ancestor lived. Check all the different locality levels, such as state/province, county, and city or township.

✓   Second: search the subject headings. After choosing a locality, try different topics to search. Some possibilities are bibliography, biography, census records and indexes, church records and indexes, emigration, gazetteers, history, immigration, land records, maps, migration, military history, minorities, social history, and tax records. Look for a list of subject headings used in that particular catalog for more ideas.

✓   Third: Author/title search. Bring a list of books that you have always wanted to consult but have never found. For author searches, there might be other titles by the same author in your area of interest.

Always make a note of the call number to save rechecking the catalog later. The library may use Library of Congress call numbers and subject headings, the Dewey Decimal Classification Scheme, Superintendent of Documents call numbers, or their own system.

If the catalog is a "union catalog," it includes resources of other libraries. A union catalog indicates who has what, including a good description of the items. A union list is simply a list by title. The most well known catalog is the *National Union Catalog* (NUC) published by the Library of Congress, and it is the most extensive list of books that has ever been published. This is one of the best sources for locating copies of books.

The *National Union Catalog of Manuscript Collections* (NUCMC) is the best source for locating manuscript collections and unpublished materials, including family collections, papers, Bibles, etc. These manuscripts are indexed in the *Index to Personal Names in the NUCMC*, 2 vols. (Alexandria: Chadwyck-Healey, 1987), and include over 200,000 names.

Academic libraries usually participate in interlibrary loan. With the use of an online catalog, such as ALADIN, DIALOG, or LOCIS, researchers can search holdings of other institutions and have books delivered on loan to their location. There is usually a fee for this service.

A college library usually has an excellent reference collection of biographical directories and indexes. Newspaper surname indexes, professional and subject biographies, and rosters or compendiums of organizations are often available. Some titles to look for are:

★ *Biography and Genealogy Master Index* (Detroit: Gale Research, 1980–). On CD-ROM and microfiche.

★ *Anglo-American Historical Names Database* (Alexandria: Chadwyck-Healy, 1985). On microfiche.

★ *Chambers Biographical Dictionary* (London: Chambers, 1978).

★ *New Century Cyclopedia of Names* (New York: Appleton, 1954).

★ *Periodicals Contents Index* (Alexandria, VA: Chadwyck-Healy, 1994–).

★ *Personal Name Index to the New York Times, 1851–1974* (Verdi, NM: Roxbury Data Interface, 1976–). There is a *1975–1979 Supplement*.

★ *The New York Times Obituary Index, 1858–1968* (Sanford, NC: Microfilming Corporation, 1970). Supplements have been published.

★ *The Dictionary of American Biography* (New York: Charles Scribner's Sons, 1977–).

Among the facilities in the national capital area are several institutions with collections that are valuable in putting together a family health pedigree. More and more genealogists are using the fields of genetics and health care to document the transmission of diseases down generational lines and record family health information.

Online databases are available for on-site searches at several libraries and by remote access. Some of the computerized services established by the National Library of Medicine (see chapter 7) are:

★ MEDLARS (Medical Literature Analysis and Retrieval System)

★ MEDLINE, the online version of MEDLARS

★ CATLINE (Catalog Online) of NLM's database

★ HISTLINE, 100,000 records of materials relating to the history of medicine

★ BIOETHICSLINE, developed and maintained by the Bioethics Information Retrieval Project and funded by the NLM

MEDLINE and CATLINE are available at more than 50,000 remote sites.

Large public and academic libraries such as the University of Maryland and Georgetown University are selected or designated depositories for U.S. government documents. The greatest advantage of this program is the access to records that are from agencies closed to the public. The Defense Mapping Agency (DMA) does not allow researchers on site, but their map collections are available for use at these institutions. Another federal agency that participates in this program is the U.S. Geological Survey.

For more information on college libraries, please consult the Association of College and Research Libraries. They provide a free service to find college and research libraries in specific areas of research.

Association of College and Research Libraries
American Library Association
50 Huron Street
Chicago, IL 60611

☎ Phone
312-944-6780

Reference publications for locating libraries and research facilities are:

★ *Directory of Special Libraries and Information Centers.* 19th ed. (Detroit: Gale Research, 1996).

★ *Directory of Federal Libraries,* by William Evinger (Phoenix, AZ: Oryx Press, 1993).

★ *Washington Area Library Directory,* by David Shumaker, ed. 2nd ed. (Washington, DC: District of Columbia Library Association, 1996).

★ *Directory of Archives and Manuscript Repositories in the United States* (National Historical Publications and Records Commission. Washington, DC: National Archives and Records Administration, 1978).

continued . . .

... *continued*

★ *A Study of Resources and Major Subject Holdings Available in U.S. Federal Libraries Maintaining Extensive or Unique Collections of Research Materials,* by Mildred Benton (Washington, DC: Department of Health, Education and Welfare, 1970).

★ *American Library Directory* (Chicago: American Library Association. Published biennially).

Universities, Colleges, and Seminaries

American University
American University Library
4400 Massachusetts Avenue, NW
Washington, DC 20016-8046

☎ Phone
202-885-3200

Jewish Studies Program (see chapter 11)

Catholic University of America
Mullen Library
Oliveira Lima Library (located in the Mullen Library)
620 Michigan Avenue, NE
Washington, DC 20064

☎ Phone
202-319-5070 (reference)
202-319-5059 (Oliveira Lima Library)

→ Public Access
Open to the public for on-site research.

✍ Publications
General Library Handbook.
Catalog of the Olivera Lima Library: The Catholic University of America. 2 vols. (Boston: G. K. Hall, 1970).

❦ Resources Available
Holdings include over one million volumes. Online catalog ALADIN available. Not all material is cataloged in the central dictionary card catalog. Some special collections are:

★ Irish history and genealogy
★ Newspapers on microfilm
★ Over 250,000 volumes on Brazil
★ Portuguese history from the sixteenth century
★ Portuguese documents about the "nobilarias," genealogies of Portuguese nobility dating from the 1600s
★ Source material on Catholic missionary orders
★ Documents from the seventeenth and eighteenth centuries.

Dominican College Library
See chapter 11

George Washington University
Melvin Gelman Library
2130 H Street, NW
Washington, DC 20052

☎ Phone
202-994-6558

→ Public Access
Open to the public for on-site research with photo ID.

✍ Publications
Defense Mapping Agency Depository Catalog.
Gelman Library Geographic Index.

❦ Resources Available
Holdings total over one million volumes. Automated catalog on CD available. Special collections include:

★ British history
★ Icelandic studies
★ Designated depository for the DMA declassified maps and USGS maps
★ National Geographic map collection
★ Washingtoniana Collections, 1830–1979, public access terminal for *Collections: DC,* a database of historical materials concerning the District of Columbia (see also Martin Luther King Library)
★ Large selection of CD-ROMS, including the National Newspaper Index and U.S. census records

★ Russia/former USSR collection
★ History of labor and education in nineteenth-century America

Information Services 202-994-6973, a commercial search service, non-profit, fee-based; provides access to collections of Gelman Library and a national network of libraries around the country.

Georgetown University
Joseph Mark Lauinger Library
and Kennedy Institute of Ethics
Bioethics Library
37th and O Streets, NW
Washington, DC 20057-1006

☎ Phone
202-687-7452 (reference, Lauinger)
202-687-6774 (Kennedy Institute)

→ Public Access
Open to the public for on-site research with photo ID. Special Collections Division is open by appointment.

✍ Publications
Roof, Sally J. and George D. Arnold, eds. *Major Titles/Sets in Microform in the Libraries of the Consortium of Universities of Washington, DC,* 1974.

❦ Resources Available at the Lauinger Library, and Special Collections Division
Holdings include over two million volumes and an online catalog (GEORGE) containing 95 percent of books in the general collection in western languages. Special collections include, but are not limited to:

★ Local area history
★ All Jesuit province catalogs since 1814 containing primary source material, including biographical information
★ Judaica collection
★ Files on Catholic missionary groups
★ Archives of the Jesuit Province of Maryland from 1634
★ Selective depository for U.S. government documents

★ Collection of European Community documents
★ French, Spanish, Portuguese, and Italian history, maps, and atlases
★ Scheuch Collection: charters from Catalonia, Spain, dating from 1261, containing archival records of the Sala family (Barcelona area)
★ Viti Collection: history and heraldry of the Knights of Malta
★ Gonzaga Family Papers: family records form Mantua, Italy from the mid 1600s to the late 1900s
★ John Gilman Shea Collection: colonial American history and Catholic history
★ Middle East collection
★ North American Indian linguistics
★ Mexican records, 1816–1848
★ Records of the Missouri Province of the Society of Jesuits, 1830s
★ NUCMC
★ Holdings of the British Embassy Library
★ Dutch history collection
★ *Guide to the Microfilm Edition of the International Population Census Records, 1945–1967*
★ District of Columbia, Holy Rood Cemetery Records, interments 1817–1917

❦ Resources Available, Kennedy Institute of Ethics, Bioethics Library
Online catalog of holdings. Online database: BIOETHICSLINE, developed and maintained by the Bioethics Information Retrieval Project funded by the National Library of Medicine. CD-ROMS include *Books in Print, Plus.* Subject specialties include biomedicine, ethics, genetics, Judaica. Special collections include:

★ Human Genome Archives
★ Kampelman Collection of Jewish Ethics
★ Shriver Collection of Christian Ethics

Howard University, Founders Library
Moorland-Springarn Research Center
African American Resource Center
500 Howard Place, NW
Washington, DC 20059

☎ Phone
202-806-7253 (Reference)

→ Public Access
Open for on-site research with photo ID.

✍ Publications
Dictionary Catalog of the Arthur B. Springarn Collection of Negro Authors, Howard University Library (Boston: G.K. Hall, 1970).

❦ Resources Available
Holdings include almost two million volumes and over two million microforms. There is an online catalog and union card catalog available. One of the largest collections in the world with holdings on the history and culture of people of African descent. Special collections include:

★ Oral history archive of black military personnel
★ Civil rights collection
★ Newspapers on microfilm project (includes African-Caribbean titles)
★ African American history
★ Blacks in the British Isles
★ The anti-slavery movement in England
★ English, French, Spanish-Caribbean cultures
★ Brazil collection
★ District of Columbia, Woodlawn Cemetery inscriptions

George Mason University Library (GMU)
Fenwick Library
4400 University Drive
Fairfax, VA 22030-4444

☎ Phone
703-993-2220 (Special Collections)

✜ Online Services
World Wide Webb http://www.gmu.edu

→ Public Access
Open to the public for on-site research with photo ID.

❦ Resources Available
The main library has a large reference collection and an online catalog (EXLIBRIS). GMU is a designated depository for USGS maps and has the complete collection. Items in the special collection include:

★ Rare book collection dating from the fifteenth century, including U.S. history titles
★ C. Harrison Mann Collection of early Virginia maps, 1600–1920, mostly sixteenth and seventeenth centuries
★ Archives of the city of Reston, VA
★ Archives of the Northern Virginia Oral History Project: interviews of the 1940s and 1950s, indexed
★ Milton Barnes Civil War Collection of Civil War era manuscripts and letters describing action in Virginia, Kentucky, and Tennessee
★ Archives of George Mason University

University of Maryland
College Park Campus
University of Maryland
McKeldin Library
University Boulevard at Adelphi Road
College Park, MD 20742-7011

☎ Phone
301-405-9075

→ Public Access
Open to the public for on-site research. Call ahead for special collection information.

❦ Resources Available
Holdings are in an online catalog and include:

★ Marylandia department
★ UMI microfilm publications, including 900 hundred reels of the Early British Periodical Series: eighteenth- and nineteenth-century periodicals and newspapers dating from 1719
★ Hubert K. Waldorn Family Collection (1815–1962)—contains research material relating to Ireland and England in the form of records, letters, etc., of the family
★ Government map series from Scandinavian countries

★ Government depository: complete set of USGS maps, DMA maps, and foreign road maps (over 72,000 maps)
★ OSS (Office of Strategic Services) Collection from World War II
★ Architectural library with special collections of oral histories, post cards, and land use
★ East Asia Collection
★ OAS (Organization of American States) Collection

Mary Washington College
R. Lee Trinkle Library
Rare Books Room and College Archives
P.O. Box 1038
Fredericksburg, VA 22401

☎ Phone
540-654-1752

→ Public Access
Open by appointment.

❦ Resources Available
Holdings include a large manuscript collection on Virginia and the Civil War. Special items include:

★ The papers of Hamilton J. Eckenrode, Virginia state historian
★ Letters of U.S. soldiers written from Fredericksburg during the Civil War, unindexed

Wesley Theological Seminary Library
See chapter 11

PRIVATE ARCHIVES AND LIBRARIES

American Red Cross Archives
Hazel Braugh Records Center
5818 Seminary Road
Alexandria, VA 22041

☎ Phone
703-813-5380

→ Public Access
Open by appointment. Phone inquiries accepted.

❦ Resources Available
The focus of the Archives is disasters from 1881 to the present. They have recently moved the 15,000-volume reference library from their headquarters in the District to Alexandria.

Material is cataloged into chronological record groups. The first three groups (1881–1946) have been transferred to the National Archives. Records from 1947–1982 are also at the National Archives, but must be requested through the Alexandria office. Records from 1983–1986 are on microfiche, while records from 1987 to the present are in hard copy only. The staff can take inquiries and search the records for researchers. Advance notice is required to retrieve appropriate records from the National Archives.

Indexes for the first five record groups (through 1982) are available on site. These are organized by locality, place name, and type of disaster.

Personnel records are kept separately, and can be searched by staff for specific inquiries. There is a special surname index for World War I records.

Folger Shakespeare Library
Research Library
210 East Capitol Street, SE
Washington, DC 20003

☎ Phone
202-544-4600

→ Public Access
Recommended for advanced researchers only. Approval needed in advance. Must demonstrate need to use resources and meet research qualifications. For access information, please write to the Librarian, Richard J. Kuhta, at the above address.

✍ Publications
The Catalog of Printed Books of the Folger Shakespeare Library and/or *Catalog of Manuscripts . . . .* 33 vols. (Boston: G.K. Hall, 1970. Supplemented 1976, 1981).

This catalog is available at George Mason University, Fairfax, VA; George Washington University, District of Columbia; and the National Gallery of Art, District of Columbia. A complete list of nationwide subscribers to the catalog is available by mail upon request.

❦ Resources Available

The collection focuses on all aspects of sixteenth- and seventeenth-century civilization, and includes 230,000 volumes and 40,000 manuscripts dating from the fourteenth century. Items of interest include:

★ Maps of Great Britain
★ Family papers and manuscripts from the 1500s
★ Seventeenth-century immigration records
★ Eighteenth-century Caribbean records
★ English manuscript collection of family papers, letters, diaries, and account books
★ French history
★ Italian state records

The National Geographic Society

National Geographic Society Library
1146 16th Street, NW
Washington, DC 20036

☎ Phone
202-857-7783 (Reference)

→ Public Access
Open to the public.

❦ Resources Available

The Society's online catalog, ORBIS, is available on site. Holdings of the library include:

★ DMA maps
★ National Geographic Card Index, beginning in 1888; cites authors, articles, photographs, and all mentions of geographic names that have appeared in the *National Geographic Magazine*

Family History Centers (FHCs)

Annandale Family History Center

3900 Howard Street
P.O. Box 89
Annandale, VA 22003-0089

☎ Phone
703-256-5518

→ Public Access

Open to the public for on-site research. Materials do not circulate.

✍ Publications

Schaefer, Christina K. *The Center: A Guide to Genealogical Research in the National Capital Area* (Baltimore: Genealogical Publishing Co., 1996).

❦ Resources Available

Annandale FHC is one of about three dozen family history centers in Maryland and Virginia.

☞ Other Area Family History Centers in Maryland and Virginia

Annapolis FHC
1875 Ritchie Highway
Annapolis, MD
410-757-4173

Buena Vista FHC
State Route 60
Buena Vista, VA
540-261-6446

Centreville FHC
14150 Upperidge
Centreville, VA
703-830-5343

Charlottesville FHC
Hydraulic Road
Charlottesville, VA
804-973-9856

Chesapeake FHC
412 Scarborough Drive
Chesapeake, VA
804-482-8600

Churchland FHC
115 Cherokee
Portsmouth, VA
804-488-4207

Columbia FHC
4100 St. John's Lane
Ellicott City, MD
410-465-1642

Frederick FHC
199 North Place
Frederick, MD
301-698-0406

Fredericksburg FHC
1710 Bragg Road
Fredericksburg, VA
540-786-5641

Gloucester FHC
8381 George Washington Highway
Gloucester, VA
804-693-5095

Hamilton FHC
Reid Street and Old Route 7
Hamilton, VA
540-338-9526

Harrisonburg FHC
210 South Avenue
Harrisonburg, VA
540-433-2945

Kensington (Washington Temple) FHC
10,000 Stoneybrook Drive
Kensington, MD
301-587-0042

Lexington Park FHC
Old Rolling Road
California, MD
301-863-8002

Lutherville FHC
1400 Dulaney Valley Road
Lutherville, MD
410-821-9880

Martinsville/Roanoke FHC
Route 57-A Riverside Drive
Bassett, VA
540-629-7613

McLean FHC
2034 Great Falls Street
Falls Church, VA
703-532-9019

Mount Vernon FHC
2000 Mount Vernon Memorial Parkway
Alexandria, VA
703-799-3071

New River/Pembroke FHC
Route 460
Pembroke, VA
540-626-7264

Newport News FHC
901 Denbigh Boulevard
Newport News, VA
804-874-2335

Oakton FHC
2719 Hunters Mill Road
Oakton, VA
703-281-1836

Richmond FHC
5600 Monument Avenue
Richmond, VA
804-288-8134

Richmond/Chesterfield FHC
4601 North Bailey Bridge Road
Midlothian, VA
804-763-4318

Roanoke/Salem FHC
6311 Wayburn Drive
Salem, VA
540-562-2052

Seneca FHC
18,900 Kings View Road
Germantown, MD
301-972-5897

Suitland FHC
5300 Auth Way
Suitland, MD
301-423-8924

Virginia Beach/Norfolk FHC
4789 Princess Anne Road
Virginia Beach, VA
804-467-3302

Waynesboro FHC
2825 Jefferson Lane
Waynesboro, VA
540-942-1036

Winchester FHC
Apple Pie Ridge
Winchester, VA
540-722-6055

Woodbridge FHC
3000 Dale Boulevard
Dale City, VA
703-670-5977

🕐 Hours
Before going to any family history center it is
a good idea to call to find out the hours it is
open. Centers close for some holidays, mainte-
nance, or staff vacations. All centers are staffed
by volunteers.

✎ Mail Requests
Family history centers do not handle mail requests for research. For addresses of FHCs in
other parts of the U.S. or the world, call 801-
240-1430, or write to the following address:

The Family History Department
50 East North Temple Street
Salt Lake City, UT 84150

❦ Resources Available
Family history centers vary in size, physical
layout, operating hours, and book and film collections. They function as branch libraries of
the Family History Library (FHL) of the Church
of Jesus Christ of Latter-day Saints. Almost two
million items of microfilm (equal to over six
million volumes) are in the holdings of the FHL,
with an additional 5,000 added monthly. The
microfiche collection numbers about 432,000

items. Most of these circulate to FHCs. This
circulating program is designed to give individuals in areas distant from Salt Lake City
access to the collection.

Types of resources available on microform include, but are not limited to:

★ National Archives and Records
Administration microfilms
★ Over 575,000 rolls of U.S. state,
county, and city records
★ Canadian record collection of 34,000
rolls
★ British records collection of 150,000
rolls
★ European collection of 562,000 rolls
★ Scandinavian collection of 206,000
rolls
★ Latin American collection of 202,000
rolls
★ 133,000 books on microfiche
★ Public records, parish registers,
censuses, etc., of most foreign
countries
★ Church and other religious records
and archives, worldwide
★ Books on local history and genealogy
★ Published genealogies, private family
papers and manuscripts
★ Records of ordinances performed in
LDS temples

Special series on microform include:

★ The Hamburg Passenger Index
(Germany)
★ Old Parochial Register (Scotland)
★ Parish and Vital Records List
★ Householders' Index (Ireland)
★ Accelerated Indexing System's
indexes of U.S. census records
★ 1841–1891 British censuses
★ British Civil Registration Index,
1837–1983, on microfiche

Some centers have permanent collections of
microfilm in addition to those ordered on loan
by patrons. All centers have a basic microfiche
collection and the FamilySearch™ program on
CD-ROM.

FamilySearch®
FamilySearch® is a CD-ROM program that allows library patrons to quickly search through the names of millions of people. It includes computerized versions of two FHL resources, the Family History Library Catalog™ and the International Genealogical Index™. TempleReady™, Ancestral File™, Personal Ancestral File®, the Social Security Death Index, and the Military Index are separate programs in the system.

The International Genealogical Index™ (IGI)
The IGI is the largest genealogical database in the world. It contains over two hundred and fifty million names from several sources, including the following:

✓   Original or compiled records of births, christenings, and marriages that have been extracted and indexed in the Family History Department's extraction programs

✓   Group sheets submitted by LDS Church members which were submitted specifically to have proxy temple ordinances performed

✓   LDS temple records

Family History Library Catalog™ (FHLC)
The FHLC describes the holdings of the Family History Library in Salt Lake City. A large majority of the two million items of microform may be ordered and circulated to FHCs.

Ancestral File™
This program allows family-linked information to be contributed to a database by both members and non-members of the LDS Church. This information can be accessed by other researchers and retrieved by family group record, pedigree, or descendancy chart. The names and addresses of submitters and contributors are also available. The current edition contains about twenty-six million names.

Personal Ancestral File® (PAF)
PAF is a database program that can be purchased for home use. It can create a GEDCOM file that will allow information to be exchanged with most other genealogical software programs. Its function in FamilySearch is to provide a format for contributing submissions to the Ancestral File.

Social Security Death Index
Contains about forty-nine million death records reported to the Social Security Administration from 1937 through 1988.

Military Index
Contains records of United States military personnel who died in Korea or Vietnam from 1950 to 1975.

Scottish Church Records
New in 1996, this index contains almost ten million names listed primarily in Church of Scotland parish registers from the 1500s through 1854.

TempleReady™
Members of the LDS Church use this program to prepare name submissions to take to LDS temples. They perform ordinances as proxies on behalf of their deceased family members. The completed ordinances are included in the next update of the IGI.

One of the fastest ways to find out where to start is by visiting a family history center and combing the Family History Library Catalog, part of the FamilySearch program. Direct searches can be made on CD-ROM by locality, surname, or microform or computer number. The microfiche catalog is organized by author/title, locality, subject, and surname. Use of FamilySearch is free, and the information may be downloaded onto a diskette or printed for a nominal copy charge.

Also found at family history centers are the Research Outlines published by the Family History Library. They are available for many countries and all U.S. states and Canadian provinces. Also available are outlines on special topics such as *Tracing Immigrant Origins*, *U.S. Military Records,* and foreign word lists and letter writing guides.

❖ Family History Library Online

FamilySearch is not available online. The library staff at the main library in Salt Lake City can answer basic questions through the following online services:

CompuServe (research questions)
17300,3123

CompuServe (FamilySearch questions)
71520,527

Genie (research questions)
F.H.Library

Genie (FamilySearch questions)
FamilySearch

America Online
FamHisLib

Prodigy
FHLS97C to F and FHLS99B to F

Chapter 11
Resources for Ethnic and Religious Research

American Scandinavian Foundation, Washington, DC
11011 Harriet Lane
Kensington, MD 20895

☎ Phone
301-949-0819

❦ Resources Available
The foundation is a publicly supported educational organization. It publishes a monthly newsletter listing events relating to Scandinavia in the Washington area.

American University Jewish Studies Program
The American University
Massachusetts and Nebraska Avenues, NW
Washington, DC 20016

☎ Phone
202-885-2423

❦ Resources Available
Lectures, conferences, and symposia sponsored by this program are open to the public. Call for more information.

Armenian Apostolic Church of St. Mary's
4125 Fessenden Street, NW
Washington, DC 20016

☎ Phone
202-363-1923

→ Public Access
Open to the public.

❦ Resources Available
The church is an important center of cultural and social activities for the community. It maintains a thousand-volume library with holdings on culture and history. Language instruction is offered, and there is a bookstore.

Cuban Interest Section
2630 16th Street, NW
Washington, DC 20009

☎ Phone
202-797-8518

→ Public Access
Appointment required.

❦ Resources Available
The section is in the process of establishing a reference facility; they will assist in obtaining research data from Havana.

Dominican College Library
487 Michigan Avenue, NE
Washington, DC 20017

☎ Phone
202-529-5300 x 154

→ Public Access
Open to the public for on-site research.

❦ Resources Available
The library's holdings include 60,000 volumes. Subject specialties include information on Dominican missionary activities and Dominican Order activity. Catalogs of St. Joseph's Province from 1900 are available, giving the date of ordination, date of birth, and date of death, if applicable.

Embassy of Australia
1601 Massachusetts Ave, NW
Washington, DC 20036

☎ Phone
202-797-3000

→ Public Access
Open to the public.

❧ Resources Available
The embassy maintains a 10,000-volume reference library. Reference services and a specialist are available. Online database services: Legi/Slate, NEXIS, DIALOG.

Embassy of Belgium
3330 Garfield St., NW
Washington, DC 20008

☎ Phone
202-333-6900

→ Public Access
Open to the public. Call in advance.

❧ Resources Available
The embassy maintains a thousand-volume library. Holdings include newspapers, periodicals, government gazetteers, and statistical information.

Embassy of Chile
1732 Massachusetts Avenue, NW
Washington DC 20036

☎ Phone
202-659-9624

→ Public Access
Open to the public.

❧ Resources Available
The embassy maintains a 2,000-volume public reference library.

Embassy of Japan
Japan Information and Cultural Center
1155 21st Street, NW
Washington, DC 20036

☎ Phone
202-939-6905

→ Public Access
Open to the public.

❧ Resources Available
There is an online research service linked directly to Japan, which the staff can use to answer questions for researchers.

Embassy of the Republic of Poland
2640 16th Street, NW
Washington, DC 20009

☎ Phone
202-234-3800

→ Public Access
Appointment required.

❧ Resources Available
The library has a newspaper collection and a video collection, including films on Nazi war crimes.

For a complete list of embassies and liaison offices, consult the Department of State Publication No. 10226, *Diplomatic List,* available through the U.S. Government Printing Office. Please call ahead before using any diplomatic facility, as access policies change frequently.

General Conference of the Seventh-Day Adventists Archives
12501 Old Columbia Pike
Silver Spring, MD 20904

☎ Phone
301-680-5020

→ Public Access
Open to the public for on-site research.

✍ Publications
Review and Herald
Adventist Review

❧ Records Available
Archive holdings include a library of denominational history materials. Special collections include:

★ Membership obituaries (found in Adventist publications)
★ Complete microfilm collection of the Millerite religious movement from the 1830s to the 1870s. This includes records, tracts, pamphlets and other materials.

U.S. Holocaust Research Institute

U.S. Holocaust Memorial Museum
100 Raoul Wallenberg Place, SW
Washington DC 20024-2150

☎ Phone
202-479-9717 (Reference Desk)

→ Public Access
Open to the public.

❦ Resources Available

★ Oral histories
★ National Registry of Jewish Holocaust Survivors, including the names of more than 90,000 survivors and their descendants. There is a bound index.
★ Eastern European history
★ A Victims Registry is in progress and being entered into a prototype database program.

Islamic Center Library

2551 Massachusetts Avenue, NW
Washington, DC 20008

☎ Phone
202-322-8343

→ Public Access
Open to the public.

❦ Resources Available
Holdings of the library include Islamic law, history, and biography

American Latvian Association

400 Hurley Avenue
P.O. Box 4578
Rockville, MD 20849-4578

☎ Phone
301-340-1954

❦ Resources Available
The association represents 200 Latvian organizations in the U.S. and can provide information about Latvian history and culture.

Memorial Foundation of the Germanna Colonies

Germanna Community College Library
P.O. Box 693
Culpeper, VA 22701

☎ Phone
703-825-1919

→ Public Access
Open to the public for on-site research.

❦ Resources Available
The Foundation's collection is housed in the community college library. The collection focuses on history and biography pertaining to the Germanna colonies in Virginia, dating from the first German settlement in 1714, and the descendants of those colonists.

Menno Simons Historical Library

Eastern Mennonite College and Seminary
1200 Park Road
Harrisonburg, VA 22801-2462

☎ Phone
703-432-4178

→ Public Access
Open to the public for on-site research.

❦ Resources Available
A two-and-a-half hour drive from Washington, this library has a very specialized collection that is valuable to the genealogist researching immigrant German ancestors. Holdings include:

★ Germanic history and German genealogies
★ Mennonite collection
★ Anabaptist collection
★ Lutheran collection
★ Reformed Church records
★ Pennsylvania Direct Tax List for 1798
★ State and local records and resources for Virginia, West Virginia, Pennsylvania, Ohio, and Maryland

Middle East Institute, George Camp Kaiser Library

1761 N Street, NW
Washington, DC 20036

☎ Phone
202-785-0183 (library)

→ Public Access
Open to the public.

❦ Resources Available
The library has a 25,000-volume collection of Middle East history, a map file, and special collections in Arabic, Farsi, and Turkish. Online database services are available.

National Association of Arab Americans
1212 New York Avenue, NW
Washington, DC 20009

☎ Phone
202-842-1840

→ Public Access
Open to the public by appointment.

❦ Resources Available
The association promotes cooperation between the Arab world and the United States. It also sponsors programs on cultural and ethnic heritage.

Organization of American States Columbus Memorial Library
Constitution Avenue and 19th Streets, NW
Washington, DC 20006

☎ Phone
202-458-6037 (Reference)

→ Public Access
Stacks are restricted, but the facility is open to the public for on-site research. Photoduplication is done by an in-house service.

❦ Resources Available
The OAS is comprised of thirty-five member states. The over 500,000-volume reference library is one of the largest collections on Latin America, second only to the Library of Congress. Special collections include:

★   2,500 maps in an uncataloged collection
★   A forty-drawer vertical file
★   Depository for United Nations documents

★   Microfilm collection of Latin American newspapers

Scottish Rite Supreme Council Archives and Library
1733 16th Street, NW
Washington, DC 20009

☎ Phone
202-232-3579, ext 39

→ Public Access
Open to the public for on-site research. Calling ahead for librarian to do preliminary research is suggested.

❦ Resources Available
The library's collection encompasses the subject of Freemasonry worldwide. Holdings include 17,000 volumes that are readily accessible; another 200,000 volumes of older volumes are on site but not easy to use. Special items include:

★   Masonic movement in Russia in the eighteenth and nineteenth centuries
★   Masonic membership records, especially the southern jurisdiction, including birth and death dates, occupation, home address, and Masonic degrees attained
★   Database containing membership information

Sisters of Mercy of the Americas, Office of Archives
8300 Colesville Road, Suite 300
Silver Spring, MD 20910

☎ Phone
301-587-0423

→ Public Access
By appointment only.

❦ Resources Available
Records of the Order of the Sisters of Mercy are preserved here, as well as Kinsale, Ireland. The activities of the order are worldwide. Holdings of the library include books, diaries, and manuscripts.

St. Josaphat's Ukrainian Catholic Seminary
201 Taylor Street, NE
Washington, DC 20017-1097

☎ Phone
202-529-1177

→ Public Access
Open by appointment only. Call on a Monday.

❦ Resources Available
The library has a selection of historical and cultural titles.

Virginia Theological Seminary
Bishop Payne Library
3737 Seminary Road
Seminary Post Office
Alexandria, VA 22304

☎ Phone
703-461-1733

→ Public Access
Open to the public by appointment.

❦ Resources Available
Special collections on Episcopal and Anglican history. CD-ROM databases and an online catalog are available.

Wesley Theological Seminary Library
4500 Massachusetts Avenue, NW
Washington, DC 20016-5690

☎ Phone
202-885-8695

→ Public Access
Open to the public.

❦ Resources Available
Holdings consist of 130,000 volumes, including collections on:

★ Early British and American Methodism
★ Historical records of the former Methodist Protestant Church

Chapter 12
Societies and Professional Organizations with Genealogical Resources

---

Adoptees in Search (AIS)
P.O. Box 41016
Bethesda, MD 20804

☎ Phone
301-656-8555

❦ Resources Available
This is a tax exempt organization that aids adult adoptees who are trying to locate their birth parents. It maintains daily hours plus a twenty-four hour answering service.

Anne Arundel County Historical Society Library and Anne Arundel Genealogical Society
5 Crain Highway, SE
Glen Burnie, MD 21061

☎ Phone
410-760-9679

→ Public Access
Donation requested from non-members using the library.

✍ Publications
The Society has republished the *1878 Hopkins Atlas for Anne Arundel County*, with an additional index.
A list of publications is available.

❦ Resources Available
The library is located in the Kuethe Library, site of the former Glen Burnie Public Library. Holdings include 3,500 volumes, including material about Kentucky, Maryland, Missouri, New York, Pennsylvania, and New England. Special collections include:

★ U.S. census indexes through 1850

★ One hundred Society of Colonial Dames lineages charts, transferred from the Maryland Historical Society, indexed
★ Ongoing project to transcribe Anne Arundel County property records
★ Anne Arundel active cemetery records CD-ROM collection
★ Microfilm collection
★ Ordnance survey maps of West Germany and Great Britain, ca. 1985
★ Telephone book collection, ca. 1980, from West Germany, Great Britain, Switzerland, and Austria

Black History Resource Center
See chapter 8

Bethune Museum-Archives
National Historic Site
National Archives for Black Women's History
1318 Vermont Avenue, NW
Washington, DC 20005

☎ Phone
202-332-1233

→ Public Access
In October 1995 the Archives were turned over to the National Park Service as a federal repository. There is no longer an entrance fee, but an appointment is required to use the Archives.

✍ Publications
Collection listing available by mail upon request.

❦ Resources Available
The Archives is a national repository for materials on African American women's history. The

focus of the collection is primarily twentieth century, and includes:

★ The records of the National Council of Negro Women
★ Collection of materials on African American women's involvement in World War II

Calvert County Historical Society
30 Duke Street
P.O. Box 358
Frederick, MD 20678

☎ Phone
410-535-2452

→ Public Access
Open to the public for on-site research. Located in the lower level of the Calvert County Public Library.

✍ Publications
A History of Calvert County, by Charles Francis Stein (Baltimore: Schneidereith and Sons, 1977).

❦ Resources Available
Holdings include: vertical files, family papers, books, and a microfilm collection of census records and newspapers.

Daughters of the American Revolution
See chapter 5

Fauquier Heritage Society
8266 East Main Street
P.O. Box 548
Marshall, VA 22115-0548

☎ Phone
540-364-3440

→ Public Access
Open to the public for on-site research.

❦ Resources Available

★ Genealogical collection of local historian John K. Gott
★ Members' family group sheets
★ Family histories and genealogies

Historical Society of Washington
See chapter 9

Montgomery County Historical Society Library
103 West Montgomery Avenue
Rockville, MD 20850

☎ Phone
301-762-1492

→ Public Access
Fee of $2.00 charged to non-members.

❦ Resources Available
The library has a collection of Montgomery County and Maryland materials, including:

★ Genealogical files
★ Copies of early county records
★ Collections of family papers
★ Photograph collection
★ Oral history tapes

The Museum and Library of Maryland History (formerly Maryland Historical Society)
201 West Monument Street
Baltimore, MD 21201

☎ Phone
410-685-3750

→ Public Access
Fee for non-members. Telephone inquiries on weekdays only. No pens allowed in the library.

✍ Publications
Manuscript Collections of the Maryland Historical Society, by Avril Pedley (Baltimore: the Society, 1968).
Guide to the Research Collections of the Maryland Historical Society, by Richard Cox and Larry Sullivan (Baltimore: the Society, 1980).
Maryland Historical Magazine.

❦ Resources Available
Although outside of the DC metro area, this library has extensive genealogical resources. Collection strengths include the following geographical and subject areas:

★ Marylandia
★ Mid-Atlantic states
★ Washington, DC
★ New England
★ Quaker history
★ Southern states
★ Indiana
★ Arkansas
★ Illinois
★ Iowa
★ Kentucky
★ Michigan
★ Minnesota
★ Missouri
★ New Jersey
★ New York
★ Ohio
★ Tennessee
★ Texas
★ Wisconsin

Also available are special collections of:

★ Norris Harris Church Register Index of over 200 volumes of transcribed church registers
★ Manuscripts
★ Newspapers bound and on microfilm
★ Vertical files of newspaper clippings

A Selection of Maryland Historical Society Resources Available Through the Family History Library System

Maryland Historical Magazine. Vol. 1 (1906)–Vol. 68 (1973). Baltimore: Maryland Historical Society, 1906–1973. Salt Lake City: Filmed by the Genealogical Society of Utah, 1968–1969, 1976. 21 microfilm reels, computer no. 0225566.

Cregar, William F. *Index to Maryland Wills,* from cards made by William F. Cregar. Salt Lake City: Filmed by the Genealogical Society of Utah, 1949. 1 microfilm reel, 0013150. Microfilm copy of typescript at Maryland Historical Society, Baltimore. Covers years from about 1666 to 1781.

National Conference for State Societies
Longworth Building
P.O. Box 180
Washington, DC 20515

☎ Phone
202-686-6292

❦ Resources Available
The conference is a national organization that provides a local network for fifty state and five U.S. territory clubs. These clubs sponsor educational, cultural, and social events. Most have a newsletter and charge a membership fee.

National Genealogical Society
See chapter 5

National Institute on Genealogical Research
P.O. Box 14274
Washington, DC 20044-4274

❦ Resources Available
The institute holds an annual seminar at the National Archives every July. Enrollment is limited to forty. Write for an application or more information.

National Society, Daughters of American Colonists
2205 Massachusetts Avenue, NW
Washington, DC 20016

☎ Phone
202-667-3076

→ Public Access
By permission of the librarian. Call for appointment.

❦ Resources Available
Reference library of historical and genealogical materials focusing on colonial America.

The National Society of the Colonial Dames of America
Dumbarton House
2715 Q Street, NW
Washington, DC 20007

☎ Phone
202-337-2288

→ Public Access
The museum is open to the public and visitors are welcome. There is a suggested donation of $3.00.

❦ Resources Available

The Society is the national headquarters for forty-four state chapters. They do not have a research facility but will provide a referral to the appropriate state society.

A Selection of Resources of the National Society of Colonial Dames Available Through the Family History Library System

Records are maintained and published by the individual state societies. A register includes the names of members, officers, ancestors, and descendants. Some of the state records available on microform include the following:

★   Connecticut, registers, 1893–1922. 5 microfiche, 6946906.
★   Illinois, member lineage cards and marriage file cards, 1599–1950. 1 microfilm reel, 1462532.
★   Massachusetts, registers, 1917. 1 microfiche, 6046842.
★   New York, ancestor index and genealogical files. 105 microfilm reels, computer no. 0000049.
★   Pennsylvania, ancestor index. 1 microfilm reel, 1697327, item 6.
★   Virginia, registers, 1892–1930. 1 microfilm reel, 1320771, item 2.

Population Reference Bureau Library
1875 Connecticut Avenue, NW
Suite 520
Washington DC 20009

☎ Phone
202-483-1100

→ Public Access
Open to the public.

❦ Resources Available
A non-profit private library, holdings include about 12,000 volumes, vertical files, and other materials on U.S. census publications from 1930 to 1990. There is a special collection on migration studies.

Prince William County Genealogical Society
P.O. Box 2019
Manassas, VA 22110-0812

☎ Phone
703-754-2234

✍ Publications
Kindred Spirits, a newsletter for members. Contains detailed updates on the RELIC holdings at Bull Run Regional Library.

❦ Resources Available
Monthly meetings are held at Bull Run Regional Library, Manassas. Visitors are welcome to attend and hear the guest speakers.

Society of the Cincinnati Anderson House Museum/Library
2118 Massachusetts Avenue, NW
Washington, DC 20009

☎ Phone
202-785-2040

→ Public Access
Prior appointment required.

❦ Resources Available
The General Society of the Cincinnati was founded in 1783. In addition to the museum, the Society maintains a 30,000-volume library with holdings pertaining to the American Revolution. Items of interest include:

★   U.S. and British regimental histories
★   Private papers
★   Muster rolls
★   Orderly books
★   Manuscript collection pertaining to the Revolutionary War period

Special Libraries Association
1700 18th Street, NW
Washington, DC 20009-2508

☎ Phone
202-234-4700

→ Public Access

Open to the public. Telephone reference service available.

✍ Publications

Information Resources Center.

❦ Resources Available

The SLA is an international organization of library professionals based in Washington, DC. The Information Resources Center will assist the public by providing information regarding special collections of any of their member libraries.

An on-site reference collection is available for consultation, including the *Washington Area Library Directory,* by the District of Columbia Library Association, and *Directory of Special Libraries and Information Centers,* by Gale Research.

Geographical Cross-Reference

Alexandria, VA
Alexandria Black History Resource Center
Alexandria Public Library, Lloyd House
   Branch
American Red Cross Archives
Mount Vernon Family History Center
Virginia Theological Seminary

Annandale, VA
Annandale Family History Center

Annapolis, MD
Annapolis Family History Center
Maryland Commission on Afro American
   History and Culture
Maryland State Archives
Maryland State Law Library
United States Naval Academy Archives
United States Naval Institute

Arlington, VA
Arlington County Public Library, Virginia
   Room
Arlington National Cemetery
Foreign Service Institute
National Genealogical Society

Baltimore, MD
Museum and Library of Maryland History

Bassett, VA
Martinsville/Roanoke Family History Center

Bethesda, MD
Adoptees in Search
National Library of Medicine

Buena Vista, VA
Buena Vista Family History Center

California, MD
Lexington Park Family History Center

Carlisle, PA
U.S. Army Military History Institute

Centreville, VA
Centreville Family History Center

Charlottesville, VA
Charlottesville Family History Center

Chesapeake, VA
Chesapeake Family History Center

College Park, MD
National Archives at College Park, Archives
   II
University of Maryland, McKeldin Library

Culpeper, VA
Culpeper Town and County Library
Memorial Foundation of the Germanna
   Colonies

Dale City, VA
Woodbridge Family History Center

Ellicott City, MD
Columbia Family History Center
Howard County Public Library

Fairfax, VA
Fairfax City Regional Library, Virginia Room
Fairfax County Publications Center
George Mason University, Fenwick Library

Falls Church, VA
McLean Family History Center

Fort Belvoir, VA
Army Engineer Museum

Fort Myer, VA
The Old Guard Museum

Frederick, MD
C. Burr Artz Library, Maryland Room
Calvert County Historical Society
Frederick Family History Center

Fredericksburg, VA
Central Rappahannock Regional Library
Fredericksburg Family History Center
Fredericksburg National Military Park
Mary Washington College, R. Lee Trinkle
   Library

Germantown, MD
Seneca Family History Center

Glen Burnie, MD
Anne Arundel County Historical Society
Anne Arundel Genealogical Society

Gloucester, VA
Gloucester Family History Center

Hamilton, VA
Hamilton Family History Center

Harper's Ferry, WV
Harpers Ferry National Historic Park
National Park Service History Collection

Harrisonburg, VA
Harrisonburg Family History Center
Menno Simons Historical Library

Hyattsville, MD
Archdiocese of Washington (Roman
   Catholic)
Prince George's County Memorial Library

Kensington, MD
American Scandinavian Foundation
Washington, DC Temple Family History
   Center

La Plata, MD
Charles County Community College,
   Southern Maryland Studies Center
Charles County Public Library

Leesburg, VA
Thomas Balch Public Library

Lutherville, MD
Lutherville Family History Center

Manassas, VA
Bull Run Regional Library
Manassas National Battlefield Park
Prince William County Genealogical Society

Marshall, VA
Fauquier Heritage Society

Mason Neck, VA
Gunston Hall Library

Midlothian, VA
Richmond/Chesterfield Family History
   Center

Newport News, VA
Newport News Family History Center

Oakton, VA
Oakton Family History Center

Pembroke, VA
New River/Pembroke Family History Center

Portsmouth, VA
Churchland Family History Center

Reston, VA
Geological Survey Library

Richmond, VA
Richmond Family History Center
Virginia State Library and Archives

Rockville, MD
American Latvian Association
Montgomery County Historical Society
   Library
Rockville Regional Library

Salem, VA
Roanoke/Salem Family History Center

Salisbury, MD
Wicomico County Free Library

Sharpsburg, MD
Antietam National Battlefield

Silver Spring, MD

General Conference of the Seventh-Day
Adventists Archives
Sisters of Mercy of the Americas, Office of
Archives

Springfield, VA

Bureau of Land Management, Eastern States
Office

Suitland, MD

Census Bureau Library
Suitland Family History Center

Virginia Beach, VA

Virginia Beach/Norfolk Family History
Center

Washington, DC

Air Force, Center For Air Force History
Library
American Battle Monuments Commission
American University
Armenian Apostolic Church of St. Mary's
Bethune Museum and Archives
Bureau of Indian Affairs, Tribal Enrollment
Service
Bureau of the Census, Census Bureau Library
Catholic University of America
Coast Guard Historian's Office
Commerce Department Library
Congressional Cemetery
Cuban Interest Section
Department of Defense Still Media Records
Center
Department of Interior Library
Department of State, Public Affairs Office
and Bureau of Consular Affairs
Department of Veterans Affairs, National
Cemetery System
District of Columbia, Department of Health
and Human Services
District of Columbia, Register of Deeds
District of Columbia, Superior Court
District of Columbia, Vital Records Branch
Dominican College Library
Embassy of Australia
Embassy of Chile
Embassy of Japan
Embassy of the Republic of Poland
Episcopal Diocese of Washington
Folger Shakespeare Library

George Washington University, Gelman
Library
Georgetown University, Lauinger Library
Glenwood Cemetery
Historical Society of Washington
The Holocaust Museum
Howard University
Islamic Center Library
Kennedy Institute of Ethics, Bioethics
Library
Library of Congress
Marine Corps Historical Center
Martin Luther King Memorial Library
Middle East Institute, George Camp Kaiser
Library
Mount Olivet Cemetery
National Air and Space Museum
National Archives and Records
Administration
National Association of Arab Americans
National Conference for State Societies
National Geographic Society Library
National Guard Association Library
National Museum of American History
National Society, Colonial Dames of America
National Society, Daughters of American
Colonists
National Society, Daughters of the American
Revolution
Naval Military Personnel Command
Navy Department Library
Navy Historical Center
Navy Memorial
Navy, Office of Public Information, Casual-
ties Assistance Branch
Oak Hill Cemetery
Organization of American States, Columbus
Memorial Library
Prospect Hill Cemetery
Rock Creek Cemetery
St. Josaphat's Ukrainian Catholic Seminary
Scottish Rite Supreme Council, Archives and
Library
Smithsonian Institution, Dwight D.
Eisenhower Institute for Historical
Research
Society of the Cincinnati, Anderson House
Museum and Library
Special Libraries Association
U.S. District Court, Clerk
U.S. Government Printing Office

Vietnam Veterans Memorial
Wesley Theological Seminary
Woodrow Wilson Center for International
    Scholars

Waynesboro, VA
Waynesboro Family History Center

Winchester, VA
Handley Public Library, Archives Room
Winchester Family History Center
Winchester-Frederick County Historical
    Society

Bibliography

ADC's Pocket Atlas of Washington, DC, and Vicinity. 2nd ed. Alexandria, VA: ADC of Alexandria, n.d.

U.S. Naval History Division. *U.S. Naval History Sources in the Washington Area, and Suggested Research Subjects.* Compiled by Dean C. Allard and Betty Bern. Washington, DC, 1976.

American Library Directory. Chicago: American Library Association. Published biennially.

American Memorials and Overseas Military Cemeteries. Washington, DC: American Battle Monuments Commission, 1994.

American Newspapers, 1821 to 1936. (1936). Reprint, Millwood, NY: Kraus Reprint Co., 1970.

American State Papers. 38 vols. Washington, DC: Gales and Seaton, 1832–1861.

Balhuzen, Anne Ross. *Searching on Location: Planning a Research Trip.* Salt Lake City: Ancestry, 1992.

Barnes, Robert. *Guide to Research in Baltimore City and County.* 2nd ed. Silver Spring, MD: Family Line Publications, 1993.

Bentley, Elizabeth P. *The Genealogist's Address Book.* 3rd ed. Baltimore: Genealogical Publishing Co., 1995 (or current edition).

Benton, Mildred. *A Study of Resources and Major Subject Holdings Available in U.S. Federal Libraries Maintaining Extensive or Unique Collections of Research Materials.* Washington, DC: Department of Health, Education and Welfare, 1970.

Biography and Genealogy Master Index. Detroit: Gale Research, 1980–.

Bockstruck, Lloyd. "Four Centuries of Genealogy: An Historical Overview." *RQ,* Winter (1983): 162–170.

Brigham, Clarence Saunders. *History and Bibliography of American Newspapers, 1690 to 1820.* 2 vols. Worcester, MA: American Antiquarian Society, 1974–75.

Burek, Deborah, ed. *Cemeteries of the United States.* Detroit: Gale Research, 1994.

Burek, Deborah, ed. *Encyclopedia of Associations.* 26th ed. 2 vols. Detroit: Gale Research, 1991.

Callahan, Edward W., ed. *List of Officers of the Navy of the United States and of the Marine Corps, from 1775 to 1900.* New York: L.R. Hamersly and Co., 1901.

Catalog of the Bureau of the Census Library. Boston: G.K. Hall, 1976.

Catalog of the Olivera Lima Library: The Catholic University of America. 2 vols. Boston: G. K. Hall, 1970.

The Catalog of Printed Books of the Folger Shakespeare Library and/or Catalog of Manuscripts . . . . 33 vols. Boston: G.K. Hall, 1970. Supplemented 1976, 1981.

Chambers Biographical Dictionary. London: Chambers Publishing, 1978.

Cobb, David A. *Guide to U.S. Map Resources.* Chicago: American Library Association, 1990.

Continental Congress. *Index and Journals of the Continental Congress, 1774–1789.* Compiled by Kenneth E. Harris and Steven D. Tilley. Washington, DC, 1976.

Continental Congress. *Journals of the Continental Congress, 1774–1789.* Edited by Worthington C. Ford, et al. 34 vols. Washington, DC, 1904–37.

Cook, Eleanor V. *Guide to the Records of Your DC Ancestors.* Silver Spring, MD: Family Line Publications, 1987.

Crowe, Elizabeth P. *Genealogy Online: Researching Your Roots.* New York: Windcrest/McGraw Hill, 1995.

Deputy, Marilyn, and Pat Barben. *Register of Federal United States Military Records: A Guide to Manuscript Sources at the Genealogical Library, Salt Lake City, and the National Archives in Washington, DC.* 3 vols. Bowie, MD: Heritage, 1986.

Dictionary Catalog of the Arthur B. Springarn Collection of Negro Authors, Howard University Library. Boston: G.K. Hall, 1970.

The Dictionary of American Biography. New York: Charles Scribner's Sons, 1977–.

Dillon, Kenneth J. *Scholar's Guide to Washington, DC for Central Eurasian and East European Studies.* Washington, DC: Smithsonian Institution Press, 1980.

Directory of Directories. Detroit: Gale Research, 1977–.

Dorr, Steven R. *Scholar's Guide to Washington, DC for Middle Eastern Studies*. Washington, DC: Smithsonian Institution Press, 1987.

Dyer, Frederick H. *A Compendium of the War of the Rebellion: Compiled and Arranged from Official Records of the Federal and Confederate Armies, Reports of the Adjutant Generals of the Several States, the Army Registers and Other Reliable Documents and Sources*. Morningside Edition. Dayton, OH: Press of Morningside Bookshop, 1978.

Eichholz, Alice, ed. *Ancestry's Red Book*. Revised ed. Salt Lake City: Ancestry, 1992.

Everton, George B. *The Handy Book for Genealogists: United States of America*. 8th ed. Logan, UT: Everton Publishers, 1991.

Evinger, William. *Directory of Federal Libraries*. Phoenix, AZ: Oryx Press, 1993.

Family History Library. *Military Records*. Salt Lake City: The Church of Jesus Christ of Latter-day Saints, 1993.

Federal Writers' Project. *Washington, City and Capital*. Washington, DC: American Guide Series, 1937.

Filby, P. William. *Directory of American Libraries with Genealogical or Local History Collections*. Wilmington, DE: Scholarly Resources, 1988.

_____. *Passenger and Immigration Lists Bibliography 1538–1900: Being a Guide to Published Lists of Arrivals in the United States and Canada*. 2nd ed. Detroit: Gale Research, 1988.

Filby, P. William, and Mary K. Meyer. *Passenger and Immigration Lists Index*. 3 vols. plus Supplements. Detroit: Gale Research, 1981–.

Fisher, Perry. G. *Materials for the Study of Washington: A Selected Annotated Bibliography*. Washington, DC: George Washington University, n.d.

Froneck, Thomas, ed. *An Illustrated History of the City of Washington by the Junior League of Washington*. New York: Wings Books, 1977.

Glazier, Ira A. *Migration from the Russian Empire*. Baltimore: Genealogical Publishing Co., 1995–.

Glazier, Ira A., and P. William Filby. *Germans to America*. Wilmington, DE: Scholarly Resources, 1989–.

_____. *Italians to America*. Wilmington, DE: Scholarly Resources, 1992–.

Glazier, Ira A., and Michael Tepper. *The Famine Immigrants*. Baltimore: Genealogical Publishing Co., 1983–.

Grant, Steven A. *Scholar's Guide to Washington, DC for Russian, Central, and Baltic Studies*. 3rd ed. Revised by William E. Pomerantz. Washington, DC: Woodrow Wilson Center Press, 1994.

Greenwood, Val. *The Researcher's Guide to American Genealogy*. 2nd ed. Baltimore: Genealogical Publishing Co., 1990.

Grow, Michael. *Scholar's Guide to Washington, DC for Latin American and Caribbean Studies*. 2nd ed. Revised by Craig VanGrasstek. Washington, DC: Woodrow Wilson Center Press, 1992.

Guide to the Resources of the United States Air Force Historical Research Center. Montgomery AL: Maxwell Air Force Base, 1983.

A Guide to the U.S. Army Military History Institute. Carlisle Barracks, PA, n.d.

Hamer, Philip, M. *A Guide to Archives and Manuscripts in the United States*. New Haven: Yale University Press, 1961.

Harris, Sherwood. *The New York Public Library Book of How and Where to Look It Up*. New York: Prentice Hall, 1991.

Hefner, Loretta I. *The WPA Historical Records Survey: A Guide to the Unpublished Inventories, Indexes, and Transcripts*. Chicago: Society of American Archivists, 1980.

Heitman, Francis Bernard. *Historical Register of Officers in the Continental Army During the War of the Revolution, April 1775, to December 1783*. Washington, DC, 1914.

Hill, Edward E., comp. *Guide to the Records in the National Archives Relating to American Indians*. Washington, DC, 1981.

Hilton, Suzanne. "The First Landowners of Washington, DC." *Heritage Quest* 55 (1994): 67–79.

Horowitz, Lois. *A Bibliography of Military Name Lists From Pre-1675 to 1900: A Guide to Genealogical Sources*. Metuchen, NJ: Scarecrow Press, 1990.

Hummel, Ray Orvin, ed. *A List of Places Included in Nineteenth Century Virginia Directories*. Richmond, VA: Virginia State Library, 1960.

Index to Personal Names in the National Union Catalog of Manuscript Collections. 2 vols. Alexandria: Chadwyck-Healy, 1987.

Johnson, Maize, comp. *National Archives Records of the U.S. Marine Corps.* Washington, DC, 1970.

Kaminkow, Marion J. *Genealogies in the Library of Congress.* 2 vols. Baltimore: Magna Carta Book Co., 1971. Supplements published 1977, 1989, 1992.

_____. *U.S. Local Histories in the Library of Congress.* 5 vols. Baltimore: Magna Carta Book Co., 1975.

Katz, William A. *Introduction to Reference Work.* Volume 1*: Basic Information Sources.* New York: McGraw Hill, 1987.

Kemp, Thomas J. *International Vital Records Handbook.* 3rd ed. Baltimore: Genealogical Publishing Co., 1994 (or current edition).

Kirkham, E. Kay. *An Index to Some of the Bibles and Family Records of the United States.* Logan, UT: Everton Publishers, 1984.

_____. *An Index to Some of the Family Records of the Southern States.* Logan, UT: Everton Publishers, 1979.

_____. Survey of American Church Records: Major Denominations in the United States Before 1880. 2 vols. Logan, UT: Everton, 1969, 1971.

Library of Congress. *Census Library Project: National Censuses and Vital Statistics in Europe, 1918–1939: An Annotated Bibliography, with 1940–1948 Supplement.* Prepared by Henry J. Dubester. Detroit: Gale Research, 1967.

_____. *A Check List of American Eighteenth Century Newspapers in the Library of Congress, 1704–1820.* Compiled by John Van Ness Ingram. Washington, DC, 1984.

_____. *Chronological Index of Newspapers for the Period 1801–1952 in the Collections of the Library of Congress.* Compiled by Paul E. Swigart. Washington, DC, 1956.

_____.*Genealogical Research at the Library of Congress.* Washington, DC, 1992.

_____. *Information for Researchers: Using the Library of Congress.* Washington, DC, 1995.

_____. *A List of Geographical Atlases in the Library of Congress: With Bibliographical Notes.* Compiled under the direction of Philip Lee Phillips. Washington, DC, 1965.

_____. *Newspapers in Microform: Foreign Countries, 1948–1983.* Washington, DC, 1984.

_____. *Newspapers in Microform: United States, 1948–1983.* Washington, DC, 1984.

_____. *Reference Services and Facilities of the Local History and Genealogy Reading Room.* Washington, DC, 1994.

Mann, Thomas. *Doing Research at the Library of Congress: A Guide to Subject Searching in a Closed Stacks Library.* Washington, DC: Library of Congress, 1994.

_____. *A Guide to Library Research Methods.* New York: Oxford University Press, 1987.

Maryland State Archives. *A Guide to the Index Holdings at the Maryland State Archives.* Annapolis, 1972, 1988 Appendix.

_____. *Researching Black Families at the Maryland State Archives.* Annapolis, 1984.

Maryland State Law Library. *Sources of Basic Genealogical Research in the Maryland State Law Library: A Sampler.* Annapolis, 1988.

McGinnis, Carol. *Virginia Genealogy: Sources and Resources.* Baltimore: Genealogical Publishing Co., 1993.

McMullin, Philip. *Grassroots of America, a Computerized Index to American State Papers: Land Grants and Claims, 1789–1837.* Salt Lake City: Gendex, 1972.

Mead, Elizabeth W., Emil Fossan, and Roger Thomas, eds. *Calendar of Maryland State Papers: No. 1: The Black Books.* Baltimore: Genealogical Publishing Co., 1967.

Meyer, Mary Keysor, ed. *Meyer's Directory of Genealogical Societies in the U.S. and Canada.* 7th ed. Mount Airy, MD: the author, 1988 (or current edition).

Morse, Richard. *Personal Papers in the United States Historical Center.* Washington, DC: 1990.

Morton Allan Directory of European Passenger Steamship Arrivals (1931). Reprinted Baltimore: Genealogical Publishing Co., 1987.

National Archives and Records Administration. *American Indians: A Select Catalog of National Archives Microfilm Publications.* Washington, DC, 1984.

_____. *Black Studies: A Select Catalog of National Archives Microfilm Publications.* Washington, DC, 1984.

_____. *Guide to Genealogical Research in the National Archives.* Washington, DC, 1985.

_____. *Immigrant and Passenger Arrivals: A Select Catalog of National Archives Microfilm Publications.* 2nd ed. Washington, DC, 1991.

_____. *List of Cartographic Records of the General Land Office* (SL 19). Compiled by Laura E. Kelsay. Washington, DC, 1964.

_____. *Military Service Records: A Select Catalog of National Archives Microfilm Publications.* Washington, DC, 1985.

_____. *1972 Census Information.* Washington, DC, 1972.

_____. *Preliminary Inventory of the Cartographic Records of the Bureau of the Census.* Compiled by James B. Rhoads and Charlotte M. Ashby. No. 103. Washington, DC, 1958.

National Historical Publications and Records Commission. *Directory of Archives and Manuscript Repositories in the United States.* Washington, DC, 1978.

National Inventory of Documentary Sources in the United States. Alexandria: Chadwyck-Healy, 1985.

National Society of the Daughters of the American Revolution. *DAR Library Catalog.* Volume 1: *Family Histories and Genealogies.* Compiled Under the Supervision of Carolyn Leopold Michaels and Kathryn G. Scott. Washington, DC: the Society, 1982.

_____. *DAR Library Catalog.* Volume 2: *State and Local Histories and Records.* Compiled Under the Supervision of Eric G. Grundset and Ana Antolin. Washington, DC: the Society, 1989.

_____. *DAR Library Catalog.* Volume 3: *Acquisitions, 1985–1991.* Compiled Under the Supervision of Eric G. Grundset and Bebe Mutz. Washington, DC: the Society, 1992.

_____. *Index of the Rolls of Honor in the Lineage Books of the National Society of the Daughters of the American Revolution.* 4 vols (1916–1940). Reprinted Baltimore: Genealogical Publishing Co., 1980.

Neagles, James C. *U. S. Military Records: A Guide to Federal and State Sources.* Salt Lake City: Ancestry, 1994.

_____. *The Library of Congress: A Guide to Genealogical and Historical Research.* Salt Lake City: Ancestry, 1990.

New Century Cyclopedia of Names. New York: Appleton, 1954.

The New York Times Obituary Index, 1858–1968. Sanford, NC: Microfilming Corporation, 1970.

Noble, Dennis L., comp. *Historical Register, U.S. Revenue Cutter Service Officers, 1790–1914.* Washington, DC: Coast Guard Historian's Office, 1990.

Nugent, Nell Marion. *Cavaliers and Pioneers: Abstracts of Virginia Land Patents and Grants.* 3 vols. Richmond, VA: Virginia State Library, 1934–1979.

Ostrow, Stephen E., and Robert Zich. *Research Collections in the Information Age: The Library of Congress Looks to the Future.* Washington, DC, 1990.

Papenfuse, Edward C., Susan A. Collins, and Christopher N. Allan. *A Guide to the Maryland Hall of Records: Local, Judicial and Administrative Records on Microform.* Annapolis, 1978.

Pazek, Lawrence J. *United States Air Force History: A Guide to Documentary Sources.* Washington, DC: 1973.

Periodicals Contents Index. Alexandria, VA: Chadwyck-Healy, 1994–.

Personal Name Index to The New York Times, 1851–1974. Verdi, NM: Roxbury Data Interface, 1976–.

Price, Robert L., ed. *The Washington Post Guide to Washington.* 2nd ed. New York: McGraw Hill, 1989.

Radoff, Morris Leon. *The County Courthouses and Records of Maryland.* Part One: *The Courthouses.* Annapolis: Hall of Records Commission, 1960.

Radoff, Morris Leon, Gust Skordas, Phebe R. Jacobsen. *The County Courthouses and Records of Maryland.* Part Two: *The Records.* Annapolis: Hall of Records Commission, 1963.

Reinhart, M. Ann. "The Challenges of Genealogical Reference Services: An Introduction." *RQ,* Winter (1983): 159–210.

Roof, Sally J. and George D. Arnold, eds. *Major Titles/Sets in Microform in the Libraries of the Consortium of Universities of Washington, DC.* Boston: G.K. Hall, 1974.

Ross, Betty. *Washington, DC Museums: A Ross Guide.* Washington, DC: Americana Press, 1992.

Schubert, Frank N., ed. *The Nation Builders: A Sesquicentennial History of the Corps of Topographical Engineers.* Fort Belvoir, VA: Office of History, U.S. Army Corps of Engineers, 1988.

Shumaker, David, ed. *Washington Area Library Directory.* Washington, DC: District of Columbia Library Association, 1992.

Schweitzer, George K. *Revolutionary War Genealogy.* Knoxville, TN: the author, 1982.

_____. *Civil War Genealogy.* Knoxville, TN: the author, 1981.

_____. *Maryland Research.* Knoxville, TN: the author, 1991.

_____. *Virginia Research.* Knoxville, TN: the author, 1982.

Smithsonian Institution. *Handbook of North American Indians.* Washington, DC, various years.

Stampp, Kenneth M., ed. *Records of Ante-Bellum Southern Plantations from the Revolution Through the Civil War: Series C, Selections from Holdings of the Library of Congress.* Frederick, MD: University Publications of America, 1985.

The Standard Periodical Directory, 1983–84. 8th rev. ed. New York: Oxbridge Communications, 1982.

Stemmons, John D., and E. Diane Stemmons, comps. *The Cemetery Record Compendium: Comprising a Directory of Cemetery Records and Where They May Be Located.* Logan, UT: Everton Publishers, 1979.

_____. *The Vital Record Compendium.* Logan, UT: Everton Publishers, 1979.

Subject Directory of Special Libraries and Information Centers, and Research Centers Directory. Detroit: Gale Research, published biennially.

Szucs, Loretto D. *The Archives: A Guide to the National Archives Field Branches.* Salt Lake City: Ancestry, 1988.

Tepper, Michael. *American Passenger Arrival Records.* Updated and enlarged ed. Baltimore: Genealogical Publishing Co., 1993.

Ulrich's International Periodicals Directory. 22nd ed. 2 vols. New York: R. R. Bowker, 1983, published biennially.

U.S. Naval History Division. *U.S. Naval History Sources in the United States.* Washington, DC, 1979.

Utah State University. *Name Index to the Library of Congress Collection of Mormon Diaries.* Compiled by the Special Collections Department, Merrill Library. Salt Lake City: 1985.

Vandagriff, G.G. *Voices in Your Blood: Discovering Identity through Family History.* Kansas City: Andrews and McMeel, 1993.

Virginia State Library. *Guide to Genealogical Notes and Charts in the Archives Branch, Virginia State Library.* Richmond, 1983.

_____. *Guide to Bible Records in the Archives Branch, Virginia State Library.* Richmond, 1985.

_____. *Guide to the Church Records in the Archives Branch, Virginia State Library.* Richmond, 1985.

Walsh. Barbara B. *Telephone and City Directories in the Library of Congress: A Finding Guide.* Washington, DC, 1994.

Wehmann, Howard H., comp. *A Guide to Pre-Federal Records in the National Archives.* Washington, DC, 1989.

White, Virgil. *Genealogical Abstracts of Revolutionary War Pension Files.* 4 vols. Waynesboro, TN: National Historical Publishing, 1990–92.

Whitelely, Sandy, ed. *American Library Association Guide to Information Access.* New York: Random House, 1994.

Winklebeck, Julie, ed. *Gale Directory of Publications and Broadcast Media.* 3 vols. Detroit: Gale Research, published annually.

APPENDIX

Selected National Archives
Order Forms

ORDER FOR COPIES OF CENSUS RECORDS

DATE RECEIVED IN NNRG

INDICATE BELOW THE METHOD OF PAYMENT PREFERRED.

☐ **CREDIT CARD** *(VISA or MasterCard) for IMMEDIATE SHIPMENT of copies*

Account Number: | | | | | | | | | | | | | | | | | Exp. Date: | Signature | Daytime Phone:

☐ **BILL ME** *(No credit card)*

REQUIRED MINIMUM IDENTIFICATION OF ENTRY - MUST BE COMPLETED OR YOUR ORDER CANNOT BE SERVICED

1. CENSUS YEAR

2. STATE OR TERRITORY

3. COUNTY

4. TOWNSHIP OR OTHER SUBDIVISION

5. NAME OF HEAD OF HOUSEHOLD

6. PAGE NO.

7. ENUMERATION DISTRICT *(for 1880, 1900, and 1910 only)*

PLEASE PROVIDE THE FOLLOWING ADDITIONAL INFORMATION, IF KNOWN

	NAME	AGE	SEX	NAME	AGE	SEX
8. MEMBERS OF HOUSEHOLD						

NATIONAL ARCHIVES TRUST FUND BOARD   NATF Form 82 (rev. 1-92)

DO NOT WRITE BELOW - SPACE IS FOR OUR REPLY TO YOU

☐ **NO--We were unable to locate the entry you requested above. No payment is required.**

SEARCHER	DATE SEARCHED

☐ REQUIRED MINIMUM IDENTIFICATION OF ENTRY WAS NOT PROVIDED. Please complete blocks 1, 2, 3, 4, 5, 6, and 7 and resubmit your order.

☐ Due to the poor quality of the microfilm, the pages you requested cannot be reproduced clearly on our equipment.

☐ The microfilm roll for the State and county for which you requested copies is missing and will take 1 to 2 months to replace.

☐ OTHER:

_____

_____

_____

_____

☐ **YES--We located the entry you requested above. We have made copies of the entry for you. The cost for these copies is $6.**

CENSUS YEAR	STATE OR TERRITORY
COUNTY	

MICROFILM PUBLICATION	ROLL	PAGE NO.
SEARCHER		DATE SEARCHED

Make your check or money order payable to NATIONAL ARCHIVES TRUST FUND. Do not send cash. Return this form and your payment in the enclosed envelope to:

NATIONAL ARCHIVES TRUST FUND
P.O. BOX 100221
ATLANTA, GA 30384-0221

PLEASE NOTE: We will hold these copies awaiting receipt of payment for only 45 days from the date completed, which is stamped here. After that time, you must submit another form to obtain photocopies of the record.

THIS IS YOUR MAILING LABEL

PRESS FIRMLY.

NAME (Last, First, MI)

(C148799)

STREET

CITY, STATE | ZIP CODE

NATIONAL ARCHIVES
ORDER FOR COPIES OF VETERANS RECORDS

DATE RECEIVED IN NNRG

1. FILE TO BE SEARCHED
(Check one box only)

☐ PENSION

☐ BOUNTY-LAND WARRANT APPLICATION
(Service before 1856 only)

☐ MILITARY

2. PAYMENT METHOD *(Check one box only)*

☐ CREDIT CARD *(VISA or MasterCard)* for IMMEDIATE SHIPMENT of copies
Account Number: Exp. Date:

Signature: Daytime Phone:

☐ BILL ME
(No Credit Card)

3. VETERAN *(Give last, first, and middle names)*

4. BRANCH OF SERVICE IN WHICH HE SERVED
☐ ARMY   ☐ NAVY   ☐ MARINE CORPS

5. STATE FROM WHICH HE SERVED

6. WAR IN WHICH, OR DATES BETWEEN WHICH, HE SERVED

7. IF SERVICE WAS CIVIL WAR,
☐ UNION   ☐ CONFEDERATE

8. UNIT IN WHICH HE SERVED *(Name of regiment or number, company, etc, name of ship)*

9. IF SERVICE WAS ARMY, ARM IN WHICH HE SERVED
☐ INFANTRY   ☐ CAVALRY   ☐ ARTILLERY

If other, specify:

Rank
☐ OFFICER   ☐ ENLISTED

10. KIND OF SERVICE
☐ VOLUNTEERS   ☐ REGULARS

11. PENSION/BOUNTY-LAND FILE NO.

12. IF VETERAN LIVED IN A HOME FOR SOLDIERS, *GIVE LOCATION (City and State)*

13. PLACE(S) VETERAN LIVED AFTER SERVICE

14. DATE OF BIRTH

15. PLACE OF BIRTH *(City, County, State, etc.)*

18. NAME OF WIDOW OR OTHER CLAIMANT

16. DATE OF DEATH

17. PLACE OF DEATH *(City, County, State, etc.)*

NATIONAL ARCHIVES TRUST FUND BOARD   NATF Form 80 (rev. 10-93)

☐ **NO--We were unable to locate the file you requested above. No payment is required.**

DATE SEARCHED	SEARCHER

☐ REQUIRED MINIMUM IDENTIFICATION OF VETERAN WAS NOT PROVIDED. Please complete blocks 3 (give full name), 4, 5, 6, and 7 and resubmit your order.

☐ A SEARCH WAS MADE BUT THE FILE YOU REQUESTED ABOVE WAS NOT FOUND. When we do not find a record for a veteran, this does not mean that he did not serve. You may be able to obtain information about him from the archives of the State from which he served.

☐ See attached forms, leaflets, or information sheets.

☐ **YES--We located the file you requested above. We have made copies from the file for you. The cost for these copies is $10.**

DATE SEARCHED	SEARCHER

FILE DESIGNATION

Make your check or money order payable to NATIONAL ARCHIVES TRUST FUND. Do not send cash. Return this form and your payment in the enclosed envelope to:

NATIONAL ARCHIVES TRUST FUND
P.O. BOX 100221
ATLANTA, GA 30384-0221

PLEASE NOTE: We will hold these copies awaiting receipt of payment for only 45 days from the date completed, which is stamped below. After that time, you must submit another form to obtain photocopies of the file.

THIS IS YOUR MAILING LABEL.

PRESS FIRMLY.

NAME *(Last, First, MI)*

STREET

CITY, STATE   ZIP CODE

A 307114

REQUEST PERTAINING TO MILITARY RECORDS

Please read instructions on the reverse. If more space is needed, use plain paper.

SECTION I—INFORMATION NEEDED TO LOCATE RECORDS (Furnish as much as possible)

1. NAME USED DURING SERVICE (Last, first, and middle)	2. SOCIAL SECURITY NO.	3. DATE OF BIRTH	4. PLACE OF BIRTH

5 ACTIVE SERVICE, PAST AND PRESENT   (For an effective records search, it is important that ALL service be shown below)

BRANCH OF SERVICE (Also, show last organization, if known)	DATES OF ACTIVE SERVICE — DATE ENTERED	DATE RELEASED	Check one OFFICER	ENLISTED	SERVICE NUMBER DURING THIS PERIOD

6 RESERVE SERVICE, PAST OR PRESENT   *If "none," check here* ▶ ☐

a BRANCH OF SERVICE	b DATES OF MEMBERSHIP FROM	TO	c. Check one OFFICER	EN-LISTED	d. SERVICE NUMBER DURING THIS PERIOD
			☐	☐	

7. NATIONAL GUARD MEMBERSHIP   (Check one): ☐ a. ARMY   ☐ b. AIR FORCE   ☐ c. NONE

c STATE	e ORGANIZATION	f. DATES OF MEMBERSHIP FROM	TO	g. Check one OFFICER	EN-LISTED	h. SERVICE NUMBER DURING THIS PERIOD
				☐	☐	

8 IS SERVICE PERSON DECEASED ☐ YES ☐ NO   *If "yes," enter date of death*

9. IS (WAS) INDIVIDUAL A MILITARY RETIREE OR FLEET RESERVIST ☐ YES ☐ NO

SECTION II—REQUEST

1 EXPLAIN WHAT INFORMATION OR DOCUMENTS YOU NEED; OR, CHECK ITEM 2; OR, COMPLETE ITEM 3		2 IF YOU ONLY NEED A STATEMENT OF SERVICE check here ☐

3 LOST SEPARATION DOCUMENT REPLACEMENT REQUEST (Complete a or b, and c.)	☐ a. REPORT OF SEPARATION (DD Form 214 or equivalent)	YEAR ISSUED	This contains information normally needed to determine eligibility for benefits. It may be furnished only to the veteran, the surviving next of kin, or to a representative with veteran's signed release (item 5 of this form).
	☐ b. DISCHARGE CERTIFICATE	YEAR ISSUED	This shows only the date and character at discharge. It is of little value in determining eligibility for benefits. It may be issued only to veterans discharged honorably or under honorable conditions; or, if deceased, to the surviving spouse.
	c. EXPLAIN HOW SEPARATION DOCUMENT WAS LOST		

4. EXPLAIN PURPOSE FOR WHICH INFORMATION OR DOCUMENTS ARE NEEDED

6 REQUESTER

a. IDENTIFICATION (check appropriate box)

☐ Same person identified in Section I   ☐ Surviving spouse

☐ Next of kin (relationship) _____

☐ Other (specify)

b. SIGNATURE (see instruction 3 on reverse side)	DATE OF REQUEST

5. RELEASE AUTHORIZATION, IF REQUIRED (Read instruction 3 on reverse side)

I hereby authorize release of the requested information/documents to the person indicated at right (item 7).

VETERAN SIGN HERE ▶ _____

(If signed by other than veteran show relationship to veteran.)

7. Please type or print clearly —   COMPLETE RETURN ADDRESS

Name, number and street, city, State and ZIP code

TELEPHONE NO. (include area code) ▶

INSTRUCTIONS

1. **Information needed to locate records.** Certain identifying information is necessary to determine the location of an individual's record of military service. Please give careful consideration to and answer each item on this form. If you do not have and cannot obtain the information for an item, show "NA," meaning the information is "not available." Include as much of the requested information as you can. This will help us to give you the best possible service.

2. **Charges for service.** A nominal fee is charged for certain types of service. In most instances service fees cannot be determined in advance. If your request involves a service fee you will be notified as soon as that determination is made.

3. **Restrictions on release of information.** Information from records of military personnel is released subject to restrictions imposed by the military departments consistent with the provisions of the Freedom of Information Act of 1967 (as amended in 1974) and the Privacy Act of 1974. A service person has access to almost any information contained in his own record. The next of kin, if the veteran is deceased, and Federal officers for official purposes, are authorized to receive information from a military service or medical record only as specified in the above cited Acts. Other requesters must have the release authorization, in item 5 of the form, signed by the veteran or, if deceased, by the next of kin. Employers

and others needing proof of military service are expected to accept the information shown on documents issued by the Armed Forces at the time a service person is separated.

4. **Location of military personnel records.** The various categories of military personnel records are described in the chart below. For each category there is a code number which indicates the address at the bottom of the page to which this request should be sent. For each military service there is a note explaining approximately how long the records are held by the military service before they are transferred to the National Personnel Records Center, St. Louis. Please read these notes carefully and make sure you send your inquiry to the right address. Please note especially that the record is not sent to the National Personnel Records Center as long as the person retains any sort of reserve obligation, whether drilling or non-drilling.

(If the person has two or more periods of service within the same branch, send your request to the office having the record for the last period of service.)

5. **Definitions for abbreviations used below:**
NPRC – National Personnel Records Center   PERS – Personnel Records
TDRL – Temporary Disability Retirement List   MED – Medical Records

SERVICE	NOTE: (See paragraph 4 above.)	CATEGORY OF RECORDS —— WHERE TO WRITE	ADDRESS CODE ▼
AIR FORCE (USAF)	Except for TDRL and general officers retired with pay, Air Force records are transferred to NPRC from Code 1, 90 days after separation and from Code 2, 150 days after separation.	Active members (includes National Guard on active duty in the Air Force), TDRL, and general officers retired with pay.	1
		Reserve, retired reservist in nonpay status, current National Guard officers not on active duty in Air Force, and National Guard released from active duty in Air Force.	2
		Current National Guard enlisted not on active duty in Air Force	13
		Discharged, deceased, and retired with pay	14
COAST GUARD (USCG)	Coast Guard officer and enlisted records are transferred to NPRC 7 months after separation	Active, reserve, and TDRL members.	3
		Discharged, deceased, and retired members (see next item)	14
		Officers separated before 1/1/29 and enlisted personnel separated before 1/1/15	6
MARINE CORPS (USMC)	Marine Corps records are transferred to NPRC between 6 and 9 months after separation	Active, TDRL, and Selected Marine Corps Reserve members	4
		Individual Ready Reserve and Fleet Marine Corps Reserve members	5
		Discharged, deceased, and retired members (see next item)	14
		Members separated before 1/1/1905.	6
ARMY (USA)	Army records are transferred to NPRC as follows: Active Army and Individual Ready Reserve Control Groups: About 60 days after separation. U.S. Army Reserve Troop Unit personnel: About 120 to 180 days after separation.	Reserve, living retired members, retired general officers, and active duty records of current National Guard members who performed service in the U.S. Army before 7/1/72.*	7
		Active officers (including National Guard on active duty in the U.S. Army)	8
		Active enlisted (including National Guard on active duty in the U.S. Army) and enlisted TDRL.	9
		Current National Guard officers not on active duty in the U.S. Army	12
		Current National Guard enlisted not on active duty in the U.S. Army	13
		Discharged and deceased members (see next item).	14
		Officers separated before 7/1/17 and enlisted separated before 11/1/12	6
		Officers and warrant officers TDRL.	8
NAVY (USN)	Navy records are transferred to NPRC 6 months after retirement or complete separation.	Active members (including reservists on duty) – PERS and MED	10
		Discharged, deceased, retired (with and without pay) less than six months. TDRL, drilling and nondrilling reservists — PERS ONLY	10
		— MED ONLY	11
		Discharged, deceased, retired (with and without pay) more than six months (see next item) – PERS & MED	14
		Officers separated before 1/1/03 and enlisted separated before 1/1/1886 – PERS and MED	6

Code 12 applies to active duty records of current National Guard officers who performed service in the U.S. Army after 6/30/72.
Code 13 applies to active duty records of current National Guard enlisted members who performed service in the U.S. Army after 6/30/72.

	ADDRESS LIST OF CUSTODIANS (BY CODE NUMBERS SHOWN ABOVE) – Where to write / send this form for each category of records						
1	Air Force Manpower and Personnel Center Military Personnel Records Division Randolph AFB, TX 78150-6001	**5**	Marine Corps Reserve Support Center 10950 El Monte Overland Park, KS 66211-1408	**8**	USA MILPERCEN ATTN DAPC-MSR 200 Stoval Street Alexandria, VA 22332-0400	**12**	Army National Guard Personnel Center Columbia Pike Office Building 5600 Columbia Pike Falls Church, VA 22041
2	Air Reserve Personnel Center Denver, CO 80280-5000	**6**	Military Archives Division National Archives and Records Administration Washington, DC 20408	**9**	Commander U.S. Army Enlisted Records and Evaluation Center Ft Benjamin Harrison, IN 46249-5301	**13**	The Adjutant General *(of the appropriate State, DC, or Puerto Rico)*
3	Commandant U.S. Coast Guard Washington, DC 20593-0001	**7**	Commander U.S. Army Reserve Personnel Center ATTN: DARP-PAS 9700 Page Boulevard St. Louis, MO 63132-5200	**10**	Commander Naval Military Personnel Command ATTN NMPC-036 Washington, DC 20370-5036	**14**	National Personnel Records Center (Military Personnel Records) 9700 Page Boulevard St. Louis, MO 63132
4	Commandant of the Marine Corps (Code MMRB-10) Headquarters, U.S. Marine Corps Washington, DC 20380-0001			**11**	Naval Reserve Personnel Center New Orleans, LA 70146-5000		

ORDER FOR COPIES OF
SHIP PASSENGER ARRIVAL RECORDS

DATE RECEIVED *(NNRG)*

INDICATE BELOW THE METHOD OF PAYMENT PREFERRED.

☐ **CREDIT CARD** *(VISA or MasterCard) for IMMEDIATE SHIPMENT of copies*

Account Number:

Exp. Date: Signature

Daytime Phone:

☐ **BILL ME** *(No credit card)*

IDENTIFICATION OF ENTRY

DATE OF ARRIVAL	FULL NAME OF PASSENGER *(Give last, first, and middle names)*	AGE	SEX
PORT OF ENTRY			
WHERE NATURALIZED *(if known)*	NAMES OF MEMBERS OF IMMIGRANT FAMILY		
SHIP NAME *(or Carrier Line)*			
PASSENGER'S COUNTRY OF ORIGIN			

NATIONAL ARCHIVES TRUST FUND BOARD   NATF Form 81 (rev. 4-92)

DO NOT WRITE BELOW - SPACE IS FOR OUR REPLY TO YOU

☐ **NO--We were unable to locate the record you requested above. No payment is required.**

MICROFILM PUBLICATION	ROLL	PAGE
RECORDS SEARCHED		SEARCHER
		DATE SEARCHED

☐ A SEARCH WAS NOT MADE because the records you requested are not documented in our ship passenger arrival list records. Please see the reverse of this form. Also, please see the enclosed pamphlet for further information about our holdings.

☐ A SEARCH WAS NOT MADE because insufficient information was supplied. Please see the reverse of this form.

☐ A SEARCH WAS MADE BUT THE RECORD YOU REQUESTED ABOVE WAS NOT FOUND. Please see the reverse of this form.

☐ A SEARCH WAS MADE BUT THE EXACT RECORD YOU REQUESTED ABOVE WAS NOT FOUND. We found a record that may be the one you seek. Please see the reverse of this form.

☐ **YES--We located the record you requested above. We have made copies from the record for you. The cost for these copies is $10.**

MICROFILM PUBLICATION	ROLL	PAGE
SEARCHER		DATE SEARCHED
ARRIVAL DATE		
PORT		
SHIP		

Make your check or money order payable to NATIONAL ARCHIVES TRUST FUND. Do not send cash. Return this form and your payment in the enclosed envelope to:

NATIONAL ARCHIVES TRUST FUND
P.O. BOX 100221
ATLANTA, GA 30384-0221

PLEASE NOTE: We will hold these copies awaiting receipt of payment for only 45 days from the date completed, which is stamped below. After that time, you must submit another form to obtain photocopies of the record.

THIS IS YOUR MAILING LABEL.

PRESS FIRMLY.

NAME *(Last, First, MI)*

STREET

CITY, STATE   ZIP CODE

B345675

WE WERE UNABLE TO COMPLETE YOUR ORDER FOR THE REASON INDICATED BELOW:

1. ☐   We found several entries for persons of the same name arriving at the same port during the same period. Additional information, such as age, occupation, etc., will help in resolving this problem.

2. ☐   We found the requested information on the passenger index, but we regret that the corresponding passenger list is missing. A copy of the index card is enclosed.

3. ☐   We are unable to locate the passenger list for the ship listed and have found no entry on the passenger index for the requested party at that port.

4. ☐   We examined the passenger list for the requested ship and were unable to find an entry for the requested passenger.

5. ☐   The register of ship arrivals did not show any entry for the ship named.

6. ☐   Our only passenger lists for the cited port do not cover the date that you have requested, and we were unable to find any entry on the index to the lists we have.

7. ☐   Because of the poor quality of microfilm, the enclosed copy is the best we could obtain with our equipment.

8. ☐   We are unable to fill your request because the appropriate microfilmed indexes are illegible. If you can supply additional information -- including either the precise date (month/day/year) of arrival or the name of the ship and the approximate date of arrival (approximate month/exact year) -- we will undertake another search.

9. ☐   Passenger arrival records in our custody are not complete. Fire, dampness, and other causes destroyed many records in the 19th century before the creating agencies transferred the records to the National Archives.

10. ☐   Our index to New York passenger arrivals covers the period 1820-46 and 1897-1943. We regret that we cannot undertake a page-by-page search of the lists for the period 1847-96, inclusive.

11. ☐   Masters of vessels departing the United States were not required to list the names of passengers.

12. ☐   Overland arrivals into the United States from Mexico and Canada are not documented in passenger list records.

13. ☐   PARTIAL MATCH TO THE INFORMATION YOU SUPPLIED: We found a record that may be the one you seek. Differences from the information you supplied are explained below. If you wish to order this record, please complete a new form, attach this page, and resubmit.

_____

_____

_____

14. ☐   OTHER:

_____

_____

_____

1. Type of Request:
☐ Freedom of Information Act (FOIA)   ☐ Privacy Act (PA)

2. Type or print below, the name, address and telephone number of the person to whom the information should be returned.

Name _____   Telephone number (Area code)
(   )

Address (Street number and name) _____   (Apartment number)

(City) _____   (State) _____   (ZIP Code)

3. Action Requested:
☐ Amendment (Privacy Act only)   ☐ Copy   ☐ Personal Review

4. Information needed to search for record(s):
Specific information, document(s), or record(s) desired.

_____

_____

_____

Purpose for which desired. (You are not required to state the purpose for your request. Doing so *may* assist the INS in responding.)

_____

_____

_____

5. Data for Identification of Personal Record (*Records normally cannot be located unless provided.)

*Family Name	Given Name	Middle Name
*Other Names used, if any	*Name used at time of entry into United States	
*Alien Registration number	*Place of birth	*Date of birth
Port abroad from which left for United States	Port of entry into United States	Date of entry
Manner of entry (air, sea, land, etc.)	Name of carrier (airline or vessel if applicable)	
*Name on Naturalization Certificate	Certificate number	Naturalization date
Address at time of Naturalization		
Naturalization Court and location		

6. Verification of identity:
☐ In person with ID   ☐ Notarized Affidavit of identity   ☐ Other (specify)

7. Authorization/Consent (Usually required if requesting records about another person.)
☐ I consent to allowing the person named below to see my record
☐ Authorization letter/G-28/Power of Attorney/Other (specify)

Name of person authorized to see record	Signature of person giving consent

8. Fees: I agree to pay all costs incurred for search, duplication and review of materials up to $25.00, when applicable.

Signature of requester	Date	Telephone number (Area code) ( )

GENERAL INFORMATION

Please read all instructions carefully before completing this form. *Applicants making false statements are subject to criminal penalties [P.L. 93-579.88 stat. 1902 (5 U.S.C. 522a (i) (3))].*

The *Freedom of Information Act* (5 U.S.C. 552) allows requesters to have access to Federal agency records, except those which have been exempted by the Act.

The *Privacy Act of 1974* (5 U.S.C. 552a), with certain exceptions, permits individuals (United States citizens or permanent resident aliens) to gain access to information pertaining to themselves in Federal agency records, to have a copy made of all or any part thereof, to correct or amend such records, and to permit individuals to determine what records pertaining to themselves are collected, maintained, used, or disseminated. The Act also prohibits disclosure of individuals records without their written consent, except under certain circumstances.

INSTRUCTIONS

How to Submit a Request.

Persons requesting a search of INS records under the Feedom of Information or Privacy Acts may submit the completed application to the INS office nearest the applicant's place of residence. Requests may be submitted in person or by mail. If an application is mailed, the envelope should be clearly marked *"Freedom of Information"* or *"Privacy Act Information Request."*

Information Needed to Search for Records.

Failure to identify complete and specific information desired may result in a delay in processing or inability to locate the records or information requested.

Data for Identification of a Personal Record.

Complete as much of this section as possible; otherwise, there may not be enough information to locate the record(s) you want. Normally, records cannot be located without the person's name, date of birth, and place of birth, or the person's alien registration number or naturalization certificate number. Social Security Account Number (SSAN) is required for identification of Federal Government employee records.

Verification of Identity in Person.

An individual appearing in person may identify himself by showing a document bearing a photograph (such as an Alien Registration Card, Form I-151 or I-551, Citizen Identification Card, Form I-197, Naturalization Certificate, or passport); or two items which bear his name and address (such as driver's license and credit cards).

Verification of Identity by Mail.

An individual shall identify himself by full name, current address, date and place of birth and alien or employee identification number. A notarized example of his signature must also be provided. DOJ Form 361, Certification of Identity, may be used for this purpose.

Verification of Identity of Guardians.

Parents or legal guardians must establish their own identity as parents or legal guardians and the identity of the child or other person being represented.

Authorization or Consent.

Other parties requesting non-public information about an individual usually must have the consent of that individual on Form G-639 or by authorizing letter, together with appropriate verification of identity of the record subject.

Fees.

Except for commercial requesters, the first 100 pages of reproduction and two hours of search time will be furnished without charge. There is a fee of S.10 per page for photocopy duplication. For requests processed under the Freedom of Information Act, there may be a fee for quarter hours of time spent for searches for and review of records. Search fees are at the following rates: $2.25 clerical; $4.50 professional/computer operator; and $7.50 managerial. Other costs for searches and duplication will be charged at the actual direct cost. Fees will only be charged if the aggregate amount of search, copy, and/or review fees is more than $8.00. If the total anticipated fees amount to more than $250.00, an advance deposit of all of the fee may be required. Fee waivers or reductions may be *requested* for a request that clearly will benefit the public and is not primarily in the personal or commercial interest of the requester.

Manner of Submission of Fees When Required.

Do not send cash. Fees must be submitted in the exact amount. When requested to do so, submit a check or a United States Postal money order (or, if application is submitted from outside the United States, remittance may be made by bank international money order or foreign draft drawn on a financial institution in the United States) made payable to the "Immigration and Naturalization Service," in United States currency. An applicant residing in the U.S. Virgin Islands shall make his remittance payable to "Commissioner of Finance of the Virgin Islands," and, if residing in Guam, to "Treasurer, Guam."

A charge of $5.00 will be imposed if a check in payment of a fee is not honored by the bank on which it is drawn. Every remittance will be accepted subject to collection.

Privacy Act Statement.

Authority to collect this information is contained in Title 5, U.S.C. 552 and 552a. The purpose of the collection is to enable INS to locate applicable records and to respond to requests made under the Freedom of Information and Privacy Acts.

Routine Uses.

Information will be used to comply with requests for information under the Acts; maintain statistical data required under the Acts; and answer subsequent inquires concerning specific requests.

Effect of Not Providing Requested Information.

Furnishing the information requested on this form is voluntary. However, failure to furnish the information may result in the inability of INS to comply with a request, or refusal to comply with a request when compliance will violate other policies or laws.

≏ U.S. GPO: 1988—202-041

Index

District of Columbia, 17, 19–20, 40, 50, 69, 88, 95–100, 103–5, 121
   Congressional Cemetery, 97, 100
   Department of Health and Human Services, 98
   Glenwood Cemetery, 97, 100
   Historical Society of Washington, 99
   Martin Luther King Memorial Library, 98–9, 103
   Mount Olivet Cemetery, 97
   Oak Hill Cemetery, 97, 100
   Prospect Hill Cemetery, 97
   Recorder of Deeds, 99
   Rock Creek Cemetery, 97, 100
   Superior Court, 98
   transportation, 4–6
   See also mid-Atlantic states
Dominican College Library, 113
Draper, Lyman, Collection, 60, 69, 93, 115
embassies. *See under specific countries*
England, 59–60, 62, 78, 88, 104–5, 107, 109
   See also British Isles
Fairfax County
   Fairfax City Library, 92
   Publications Center, 92
Family History Centers, 3, 38, 81, 107–10
Family History Library, 3, 38, 49–50, 62–3, 71, 73, 88, 91, 100, 109–11
FamilySearch, 3, 55, 73, 81, 93, 109–11
Fauquier Heritage Society, 120
Federal Information Center, 83
Florida, 17, 19, 37, 39–40, 43, 46–8
   See also southern states
Folger Shakespeare Library, 106–7
France, 60, 76, 105, 107
Frederick County, C. Burr Artz Library, Maryland Room, 89
Fredericksburg (city), Central Rappahannock Regional Library, 93–4
Fredericksburg Battlefield National Military Park, 80

General Conference of the Seventh-Day Adventist Archives, 114
Georgetown University, 102, 104
George Mason University, 105, 107
George Washington University, 103–4, 107
Georgia, 13, 16–17, 19–20, 37, 59, 69, 88
   See also southern states
Germany, 16, 32, 60, 69, 78, 88, 109, 115–19
   Memorial Foundation of the Germanna Colonies, 115
   Menno Simons Historical Library, 115
Gunston Hall Library, 91
Hawaii, 15, 40
Harper's Ferry National Historic Park, 80
Holocaust Museum, 115
   See also under Jewish research
Howard County Public Library, 89
Howard University, 104–5
Hungary, 16
Iceland, 103
Idaho, 40, 43
Illinois, 13, 16–17, 19, 26, 38–40, 42–3, 48–50, 69, 121–2
Indian. *See* Native American research
Indiana, 13, 17, 19, 39–40, 42–3, 47–50, 121
Iowa, 13, 19, 39, 40, 42–3, 48, 50, 121
Ireland, 32, 59, 103, 105, 109, 116
   See also British Isles
Italy, 32, 104, 107
Japan, 78
   Embassy of, 114
   See also Asia
Jewish research, 62, 104, 113, 115
   American University Jewish Studies Program, 113
   Holocaust Museum, 115
Kansas, 13, 16–18, 40–1, 50, 69, 88, 92, 105, 119, 121
Kentucky, 13, 16–17, 19–20, 25, 27, 40, 69, 88, 92, 105, 119, 121
land records, U.S.

Bureau of Land Management, 24–5, 39–43, 47, 49–50
   case files, 41, 43–8, 69
   bounty land, 7, 9, 22–6, 39, 41, 44, 70
   cash entries, 41, 43–4, 46
   credit entry files, 41, 43–4, 46
   donation files, 41, 47–8
   homestead entries, 35, 41, 43–4, 46
   maps, 41, 48–50, 53, 61–2, 76, 87–8, 90, 94, 99,101, 103–7, 116
   preemption claims, 41, 44, 46
   private land claims, 41, 44, 48
   timber claims, 41, 44, 46
   Geological Survey Library, 40–1, 102
   patents, 41, 43, 70
   public land survey system, 39–45, 84
   tract books, 41–3, 70
Latin America, 54, 83, 109, 116
   Organization of American States, 116
   See also specific countries
Latvia, American Latvian Association, 115
Library of Congress, 1, 40–1, 50–63, 98
   John Adams Building, 51–2, 62
   photoduplication service, 53, 62
   Thomas Jefferson Building, 1, 51–9
   Local History and Genealogy Reading Room, 55–7
   Main Reading Room, 57–8
   Microform Reading Room, 59
   James Madison Building, 51–2, 59–62
   Geography and Map Division, 50–1
   Manuscript Reading Room, 60
   Newspaper and Current Periodical Reading Room, 51, 60–1
Loudon County, Thomas Balch Public Library, 92
Louisiana, 16–17, 19, 31–3, 37, 39–40, 43, 46, 48, 50, 69–70
   See also southern states
Maine, 13, 19–20, 35, 37, 40, 70
   See also New England states